W9-COP-907

MARY, QUEEN OF SCOTS

MARY QUEEN OF SCOTS

BY EMILY HAHN

Illustrated by WALTER BUEHR

RANDOM HOUSE · NEW YORK

FOURTH PRINTING

Copyright 1953 by Emily Hahn

All rights reserved under International
and Pan-American Copyright Conventions
Published in New York by Random House, Inc.
and simultaneously in Toronto, Canada by
Random House of Canada Ltd.

Library of Congress Catalog Card Number: 53-6265

Manufactured in the U.S.A.

for Rupert Cooper

MARY, QUEEN OF SCOTS

The Beginning: A Baby's Crown

FIFTY YEARS after Columbus discovered America, Mary Stuart was born. That was in 1542, in Scotland, when nobody cared about Columbus or a new continent. The center of the world was Western Europe, and the baby who became a queen before she was a week old seemed far more interesting than the fate of a few Spanish ships.

Mary Stuart still fascinates the world. She was the heroine of a stupendously exciting story, which was a tragedy and a mystery all

CHAPTER ONE

The Beginning: A Baby's Crown

FIFTY YEARS after Columbus discovered America, Mary Stuart was born. This was in 1542, in Scotland, where nobody cared about Columbus or a new continent. To Scots, the world was Western Europe, and the baby who became a queen before she was a week old seemed far more interesting than did the fate of a few Spanish ships.

Mary Stuart still fascinates the world. She was the heroine of a tremendously exciting story, which was a romance and a mystery all in one. She was lovable and unlucky and the victim of world-shaking affairs. But what people remember best about her is that she was one of two great queens, rivals as different from each other as day and night. They were cousins: Elizabeth I of England and Mary, Queen of Scots.

Mary never saw her father, James V of Scotland. His army had just been defeated by the English when she was born, and he lay ill, in hiding, far from Linlithgow where her mother was waiting for him. He had hardly time to hear of his daughter's birth before he died.

Mary of Guise, the widow, must have felt lost and frightened, all alone with a new baby. But she was used to war. War between England and Scotland was nothing new, and the local struggles between Scottish chieftains didn't worry her unduly. In those days there was no such thing as war as we know it, only occasional battles, and there were not many firearms. Still, James's army had been scattered, and there was little to prevent the English forces from marching across the border all the way to Linlithgow, and taking mother and child prisoner.

Fortunately for Mary it was not considered a kingly act to take advantage of a defenseless widowed Queen Mother, and so Henry VIII, the King of England, did not send his soldiers. Instead he announced that he was extending a protectorate over Scotland. He would take possession of the baby queen, Mary Stuart, he said, and bring her up at the English Court, and marry her to his only son, Edward. Thus when Edward became King, Scotland and England would be combined.

But Mary of Guise, the Queen Mother, was a Frenchwoman who didn't trust the English, because they were traditional enemies of her country. She tricked Henry and put him off, saying that Mary was too young to leave her mother. Henry promised to wait ten years, after which, he said, the child must come to England. For the next few years everyone at the Scottish Court was constantly on the watch, fearing that the English would change their minds, and that someone might kidnap the little Queen.

From the earliest time she could remember, Mary Stuart knew fear and flight. She was only seven months old the first time she was snatched

Mary was carried off to Stirling Castle

up and carried off to a safer place, at Stirling Castle. She must have got quite used to the alarm being sounded in the dark night. The bedroom would suddenly be filled with the whispering of ladies-in-waiting in their night robes who would hurriedly dress her and wrap her up warmly. This was done under the direction of her mother—tall and calm and always courageous among the agitated women of the household. Then would come the soft, stealthy escape from the castle, and the wild flight, horses' hoofs clopping in the cold and the dark.

Linlithgow Palace, in ruins now, stands at the edge of a lake not far from Edinburgh. The rooms were spacious for those days, and splendidly appointed, but we would probably find them cold, drafty, and cramped. They were dark, though the windows were of wonderful stained glass. There was not much furniture, and what there was was massive. Tapestry, hung on the walls, failed in its purpose of keeping out wind and damp, but it gave color and beauty to the dark rooms, and hid the cold stone. Mary of Guise, like other gentlewomen, spent a good deal of time at needlework, embroidering rich stuffs for altar-cloths and bed-hangings.

The fireplaces were large enough to hold whole logs. The beds were big four-posters with roofs and curtains, so that when the curtains were drawn the bed made a little room in itself. The main bedrooms had "garde-robes," dressing rooms in which clothes were kept; some of the garde-robes had open shafts which led straight down to the ground. This was all the sanitation possessed by the wealthiest homes, anywhere in Europe. Every so often rich families like Mary's moved to another of their great houses in order that the dwellings might be cleaned and sweetened while they were away.

In Scotland the houses of the nobles were fortresses rather than simple residences, for these men were frequently at war with one another. Behind the stone walls they kept large stocks of wine and provisions. But in many of these places there was no adequate water supply. Drinking-water had to be carried in, and laundry was given to laundresses who called for the dirty linen and washed it in the village or some near-by river.

The English and Scots ate large amounts of meat and pastry, with cabbage and plenty of sweetmeats. They did not use lettuce or beets or carrots, because they had not yet learned that such things were good to eat. Plates, cups, and dishes were so rare and costly that people usually shared plates, one for every two persons. Knives, spoons, and fingers were the tools used for eating. The fork had been invented, but was used only for serving or for spearing things out of bottles.

But though eating and other household arrangements were very simple, the clothes of sixteenth-century princes were beautiful and more luxurious than anything we see today. Silks, plain and figured, satins, velvet, lace, and rich furs clothed ladies and gentlemen in the glowing colors of tropical birds.

The mistress of Linlithgow, Mary of Guise, was the mother of Mary Stuart and the sister of the French Duke of Guise. The Guise family was so strong that its members held almost as much power as the King himself. Another of little Mary's uncles was Charles, the Cardinal of Lorraine.

Mary of Guise had not been happy at leaving her French home to live in the cold, wild land of Scotland, but she never complained. The family wanted her to make this marriage because they felt it would be advantageous to the clan, and of course she obeyed. Sixteenth-century marriages were usually arranged in this fashion; few people married for love. At one time, she might have married Henry VIII of England himself. He said when he proposed the match that he was a big man who needed a tall wife, and Mary of Guise was very tall and very handsome. But Henry had a bad reputation for beheading his wives, and so she laughingly refused, saying, "But I have a slender neck." She must often have remembered this in Scotland later.

In the sixteenth century, power was greatly to be desired, for with power came wealth and glory not only for oneself but for one's whole family.

In our time we have seen more than one king give up his throne. These modern kings have made little fuss about their abdications. Sometimes the retiring monarch seems actually happy to be relieved of his position. But in Mary's time no king ever gave up his throne without making a terrific struggle to hang on to it. If he happened to be a child or a weakling, there were plenty of nobles to do his fighting for him, and to do his ruling too.

It was a simpler society than ours, and a much smaller world. The plain people did not count in political life, although as mobs they sometimes made their wishes felt. The Court handled international affairs, and the chief object of courtiers was advancement for themselves and their clans.

Yet loyalty to the throne was not completely mercenary. It was, in a way, religious. Nearly everyone believed firmly that the king was King because his blood was royal; that is, because God willed it. Sometimes people were puzzled as to why God should have chosen some particularly bad specimen. When they thought the king was too tyrannical, there was a rebellion in spite of his royalty. But even when a king had been driven out or killed, everyone was agreed that the next ruler must be someone of the king's family, someone in whose veins flowed the same royal blood.

These rebellions and wars depended on the nobles and gentry. The people were easily persuaded to believe as their leaders wished them to believe. Most of them could not read or write, and for educated people there was not much literature. Only the wealthy could afford books. Ideas were spread by public debate, and popular history was handed about by word of mouth.

In all England there were not more than four million people—in New York alone, today, there are more than that—and the population of Scotland was much smaller.

However, though Scotland was not a large nation, and though other people looked down on the Scots, and called them uncivilized, the north country was important. England, ever watchful and jealous, did not wish France and Scotland to make an alliance, what with the Queen Mother of Scotland being French and the Catholic religion holding sway in her country as it did.

Henri II, King of France, favored marrying his little son to Mary because she was Catholic. The English, since Henry VIII had broken away from the Church of Rome, were turning Protestant. This alone was enough to increase the enmity between France and England. Religious persecution was at the back of most of the European world's unrest in the sixteenth century.

Henry VIII, when he got angry with the Pope, declared England separate from the Church of Rome. But England did not turn

Protestant overnight. It takes a long time, several generations, to change a nation's religion altogether. Henry's party of courtiers liked his action because they profited by it; Henry, when he grabbed the Church property, gave them a share. But even at Court a few people were secretly scandalized and terrified by what had been done. Like much of the country they continued quietly to believe in the Church of Rome.

Besides, they looked ahead to possibilities after Henry's death. What if their next ruler should be a Catholic? Then things would be turned around. Catholics were now being beaten and tortured and put into prison or killed, but the same thing would happen to Protestants if a Catholic monarch succeeded. Protestants were being persecuted in France all the time.

People reminded themselves that the child Mary, Queen of Scots, who was Catholic, might possibly be Henry's successor. She had a good claim to the English throne. Her grandmother, Margaret Tudor, was Henry's sister. But Henry himself in his will laid down his ruling as to who should come after him, and Mary was not high on the list. First, of course, would be his only son, Edward, for boys always had precedence in these matters. Henry realized, though, that Edward was not a good risk; he was delicate and might not live to have children. So Henry said that if Edward died without children, his older daughter, Mary Tudor, should be Queen, and if she too died without children Elizabeth, her younger half-sister, was to follow.

You might think that Mary, Queen of Scots had no chance ever to be Queen of England, since Henry had three children of his own. But that is where the religious quarrel comes in.

When he had wanted to marry Anne Boleyn, Henry argued that he had never been properly married to his first wife, Katharine of Aragon, the mother of Mary Tudor. If he had been right—and the Protestant religion said he had been—Mary Tudor was not a legitimate child. Therefore, said the Protestants, she had no right to be Queen.

Mary Tudor was a Catholic, as in defense of her mother and herself she would naturally be.

So the Catholics on her side maintained that Henry had had no right to call himself married to Anne Boleyn, because Katharine of Aragon was still alive. *They* insisted that it was Elizabeth, daughter of Anne, who had no legal claim to the throne. At least neither Church could protest against Edward, because by the time Henry married Edward's mother, Katharine of Aragon was dead and Anne Boleyn had been beheaded.

People at the English Court kept an eye on all these matters. Those who were on Elizabeth's side knew that the Scottish Queen Mary's existence threatened their princess's chances. Elizabeth, who was eight years older than Mary Stuart, knew it too.

Now and then some Scots noble asked the widowed mother to marry, so that he might take advantage of Queen Mary's youth and obtain her throne for himself. But the mother remained single and concentrated all her attention on the duty of bringing up her daughter. They loved each other dearly.

Mary of Guise chose friends for the child very carefully from the Catholic families she knew she could trust. Four little girls of the same age as Mary Stuart were selected; they were all named Mary after the Queen, and they were known as the four Maries. These girls were Mary Beaton, Mary Seaton, Mary Livingston and Mary Fleming, and you will find them mentioned in many ballads and poems, for they were to remain loyal to their playmate and sovereign all their lives.

During the Queen's childhood, a governing Council had been appointed to run Scottish affairs. Mary was not quite six when her mother persuaded this Council to let the child go abroad, not to the unsympathetic English but all the way to France, her mother's country. It must have been a difficult thing for Mary of Guise to do, thus to cut herself off from her only child, but she felt she had no choice. It was her duty to Mary, who would be safer in France. It was her duty to her Church to let the child grow up in a Catholic country. And it was her duty to her own people, the Guises, for Queen Mary would marry the Dauphin, Henri's son. One day a Guise would be Queen of France.

The brave woman won her point, sent Mary off, and settled down to a lonely life, far from everyone she loved.

CHAPTER TWO

Beloved France

MARY WASN'T quite six years old when she went to France. She enjoyed the journey, but many of the grownups were seasick. The ship went the long way around by the north passage, because there was an English fleet in the Channel watching the ordinary route. It was a rough passage and an anxious one, but the little girl didn't care about that. She had plenty of friends with her—the four Maries, and her older half-brother, the Lord James Stuart.

James was the son of James V, Mary's father,

She was spirited from Scotland to France

by Margaret Erskine, who was his morganatic wife. That means she was married by special arrangement as a commoner, and the marriage was dissolved later. Kings sometimes did marry in this way, and the children by these marriages were supposed to have no claim to the throne. James Stuart was jealous of his sister for holding the position he felt was rightly his. But he didn't show his feelings.

When they landed in France the party was taken upstream on the Loire River, by easy stages, to the French Court at St. Germain. It was beautiful smiling countryside they sailed through, and the French people smiled too. Everywhere they staged celebrations to welcome the royal child. At one town she was greeted by children dressed in white and playing fiddles; it was this band that played her through the city gates.

The Court of Henri II was as different as one can imagine from Mary's Scottish home. Stirling Castle was forbidding and dark and shrouded in mist a good part of the time, but the palaces of France were sunny and warm. Life was peaceful and luxurious. The people were not grave and thoughtful as they were in Scotland; they laughed readily, and reveled in beautiful things —little finicky things, pretty books and jewels and songs. King Henri was a cheerful, active man who loved his children.

Everyone made a great fuss about Mary, and flattered and spoiled her. Her grandmother, the old Duchess, was so pleased that she wrote to little Mary's mother, "Sete petite dame [that little lady] is very pretty indeed, and as intelligent a child as you could wish to see." The King was delighted with the pretty child, and she liked him too, and prattled freely with him. The French thought it odd and charming to hear her speaking Scots. Her uncle, Cardinal Charles, said proudly that she talked with the King "just like a woman of five and twenty."

Everyone said she was beautiful. This was only to be expected, because people are ready to see beauty in royal personages which they would not observe in commoners. But Mary really was attractive. Her pictures show it, and they were painted at a time when portrait-painters did not flatter. She wasn't beautiful, strictly speaking, but she was very pretty, with ruddy-gold hair as a child (it darkened to brown later), large dark eyes, and a delicate clear white skin. She was tall and well made. When she grew up she was six feet tall. This is a remarkable height for a girl today, but it was more remarkable in the sixteenth century when people tended to be smaller than they are now. Everyone felt it was right that a queen should be so tall; it set her off as a member of royalty. (Elizabeth of England was unusually tall, too.)

All who met her agreed that Mary's personality was sweet. She was warm-hearted, and had pretty manners. She was lively and happy-natured; it is no wonder that people fell in love with her.

Among King Henri's sickly, unattractive children she must have stood out all the more. She played happily with them, especially with her future husband François, the little Dauphin, who was about a year younger than she was. There were thirty-seven children of noble families who shared the lessons and games of the King's children. With such a number, the youngsters made up a whole village by themselves. They needed half a dozen people just to look after their wine. Fifty servants worked in their kitchen. Thirty-six pounds of cutlets were eaten in one day.

They had twenty-two lap dogs and four big bulldogs, "well-muzzled." They had falcons and pet birds and all the horses they wanted. This may sound as if Mary's life was all playtime, but actually she studied and worked very hard. Girls did work hard at their schooling in the sixteenth century, and because Mary was a Queen she was supposed to be cleverer than the others. She had to learn Italian, French, Latin, and Greek. In spite of her tutors' polite reports, she was not very good at languages; her cousin Elizabeth, over in England, was much better. But Mary was not backward. Her Greek was never brilliant, but she learned Latin well enough, and Italian.

It was in other branches of learning, subjects much valued in Henri's Court—poetry, music, and dancing—that she excelled. She was not interested, as Elizabeth was, in religious arguments. Like a good girl she read all the books on religion that her uncle gave her, and memorized the principles he wanted her to imbibe.

She didn't question them or argue; such subjects didn't interest her. She preferred poetry and novels; she loved to read and write poetry.

She was good at sports, proud of her graceful dancing (dancing was a complicated exercise then), and an excellent horsewoman. She loved pretty clothes and she had plenty of jewels. Throughout her life she was always generous with her clothes and trinkets.

But she also had faults. Little Mary Stuart was greedy and loved so much to eat that if she wasn't watched, she overate. Her uncle complained that she made herself sick eating too much melon.

But childhood did not last long for queens in the sixteenth century, and Mary was only fifteen when she was married to her fourteen-year-old cousin, the Dauphin. It was a magnificent wedding, and she must have enjoyed her fine clothes and flashing jewels. She had always known she would be married to François, and because she liked him she did not mind at all, especially since she would not have to leave France, as Mary of Guise had done. For by this time, after having spent so much of her life there, Queen

Mary loved France and looked on it as her home. French was her language, and she had French tastes and ideas.

Although you might think that a queen of Scotland ought to live in her own country and rule it, Henri II, her father-in-law, would not have agreed. She was also his son's wife, and when Henri died she would be Queen of France as well as Queen of Scotland: according to the Guises she was really Queen of England as well. Queen of three countries! It was a proud position. And as no one woman could rule over all three countries at once, Mary might as well stay in France as in Scotland. Besides, her mother was in Scotland and could do the work just as well.

The Queen Mother was given the title of Regent of Scotland. In theory she was now able to rule her daughter's country. In practice, she did not find this a very simple matter, as we shall see.

Mary at fifteen seemed much older than a fifteen-year-old girl of today. In fact, it was rumored at Court that she had fallen a little bit in love with someone else before her wedding-

All of the French court celebrated Mary's wedding

day. When the news arrived that this man was marrying someone else, Mary fainted. Mary always fainted when anything upset her badly. She probably had some illness people did not know about. At any rate she showed no signs of being unhappy with François. On the contrary, she enjoyed life very much. She loved hunting and music and finery.

A girl of fifteen is easily influenced by her elders. So it was that on Cardinal Charles's advice she signed a secret agreement to leave Scotland and her English claims to Henri in case she should die without children. It was a secret treaty, but somehow secrets leak out among diplomats, and the English Court soon heard of this one. They were indignant, and their indignation waxed stronger when they heard of something else Mary Stuart did.

Mary Tudor, who succeeded to the English throne after her father Henry VIII and her half-brother Edward had died, died in her turn in 1558, soon after the Dauphin's wedding. When news of this reached France, Mary Stuart added the arms of England to her shield. This meant that she considered herself Queen of England;

it meant that Queen Elizabeth, who had just mounted the throne, had no right to be there. It was an idle piece of vanity, but it caused ill-feeling.

Elizabeth was not outdone; she added the arms of France to *her* shield.

All the time these things were happening, the religious struggle was growing fiercer. In France the Huguenots, as Protestants were called there, were terribly persecuted. When they refused to give up their faith they were imprisoned, tortured and killed, with the approval of people like the royal family and the Guises. The Princes thought the service of God demanded this dreadful work.

In England and Scotland the spirit of intolerance was just as strong but it worked the other way. Fortunately, the Protestants were not powerful enough to treat British Catholics quite so badly. However, the Protestants of Scotland were increasing in numbers and influence. The English were glad to encourage this movement, so that France's influence might be shaken off.

Lord James, Mary's half-brother, was one of

the strongest Protestants among the plotting nobles. He had been to England and talked with Elizabeth and was convinced that she would back his cause if he led a revolt against Mary; he hoped he might be King of Scotland yet.

There were other men who thought they had as good a claim to the title as James. Some of them, following his line of reasoning, deserted the Catholic faith and embraced the Protestant; but this was not true of all of them. The Lennox family, for instance, did not. They were closely related to Mary. Lady Lennox was the daughter of Margaret Tudor, Mary's grandmother. But Margaret had married twice; her first husband had been James IV of Scotland, Mary Stuart's grandfather; her second husband had been Archibald Douglas, the father of Lady Lennox. For this reason, Lady Lennox's claim to royal blood was not quite so strong as Mary's. Still, Lady Lennox did not lose hope that her son, Lord Darnley, might some day wear a crown.

All this discussion of descent and royal blood sounds dull and confusing to us of the twentieth century. That it is necessary in order to understand what followed is due in large part to a man who lived at this very time, a Scot named John Knox.

Knox was a minister who had studied under the great reformer Calvin in Geneva. He had suffered at the hands of Catholic rulers and their adherents. He had been driven out of England during the persecutions under Mary Tudor, and thrown into prison in France. The wrongs done to him had strengthened his rebellious spirit.

Like the other reformers Knox questioned the rights of earthly princes, but he went further: he particularly queried the rights of *female* princes. It enraged him that a mere woman, Mary Tudor, should have been able to send him out of England. Mary of Guise had snubbed him too, and he was sure that her daughter, being a Catholic, would be just as bad. And here was another woman, Elizabeth, sitting on the throne of England! Had the world gone mad that such a state of affairs should exist? What had caused this sudden pest of queens? God could not have intended women to rule. Knox wrote a furious article which he published in a pamphlet called "The First Blast of the Trumpet against the Monstrous Regiment of Women." Of course the royal ladies all read the pamphlet and did not love him for it.

Now Knox had gone back to Scotland, there to preach against Catholicism, especially Catholic queens. Mary Stuart had been married a year when she heard that he was stirring up serious trouble in her country. John Knox had preached a fiery sermon at Perth, and afterwards there were riots in the city. Churches were wrecked and convents outraged. It was more than enough to make the frightened royalists remember the bad old days of Henry VIII, and his sack of the churches.

The Guises might have sent soldiers to repress this movement, but their minds were elsewhere. A double royal wedding was in the offing in France. King Henri's sister was going to be married to the Prince of Savoy, and at the same time his daughter Elizabeth was marrying Philip II of Spain. France had been warring with Spain for years, and this marriage meant peace between them—and thus worry for England.

The celebrations were tremendous and continued for several days. There was a tournament, of course. On the last day King Henri participated, as he loved to do. By accident, the lance of his opponent tore away the King's visor, and a splinter from the broken lance was driven into his skull. He died, and Mary's husband François became King of France. This event kept the Guises from thinking of Scotland; they were proud and happy that their plans were working out so well for Mary. But it wasn't perfect for her.

Not quite everyone at the French Court loved Mary. No one, especially no one of eminence, can avoid making enemies, and Mary made a strong one—her mother-in-law Catherine de Medici. The two had never got on, for the strong-willed Catherine tried to bully Mary. Mary, in turn, was rude to her mother-in-law, and called her "a merchant's daughter." This was particularly cutting because it reflected on Catherine's family, the Medici, who were merchant princes of Florence. Having made their money in trade, the Medici were not entitled, according to proud Mary, to set themselves up as royalty. So Catherine had some reason to be angry. As soon as François was King, Catherine became merely the Queen Mother and had to give first place to Mary, which caused more spite than ever.

This, however, was merely a family feud. More widespread struggles claimed the attention of the young King and Queen. Protestant fervor grew. It was heightened by the sight of Huguenots being burned in the public square. Feeling ran so high that the Court was afraid of civil war, and moved to Amboise. Even there, Huguenots crowded around the Castle to attack it.

The riot was quelled by a trick. The nobles who were leaders of the mob were lured into the Castle by a promise that they could speak to the King. There they were thrown into prison and tortured, while their poor followers waiting outside were attacked and slaughtered. The next day, the leaders were brought out, hardly able to walk, and in the courtyard they were hanged and beheaded. And the whole Court watched this horrible scene, as if it were a play.

We know that the young King and Queen

were not wholly willing, for we are told that François freed forty-six of the poorest Huguenots and gave them money. Mary wept because one of the tortured men was the husband of her lady-in-waiting. But Catherine was cruel and had no objection at all to the spectacle.

With all these troubles to distract their attention, the Guises were slow in sending aid to the poor Regent struggling along in Scotland. They tried to do too much and it took too long a time. The Regent told them she didn't need much of an army to settle the Scots, because the Lords were busy quarreling among themselves and were not strong. But the Guises liked to do things on the grand scale.

They were so slow getting a big fleet together and sending it to Scotland that the English got in ahead of them. English ships were in the Firth of Forth when the French ships got there, and then a big storm blew up and scattered the French fleet. Mary Stuart, worried about her mother, wanted to collect another expedition right away, and take it over herself. But the Huguenot troubles took up everybody's attention just then, and by the time they were dealt with, the Regent of Scotland had been deposed.

She was not harmed, but she had no power. She went on living in her palace, but a committee of Protestant Lords, called "the Congregation," governed the country.

It was an open secret that Elizabeth of England had helped the Lords to throw the Regent over. In many ways the English Queen wasn't in her heart on the side of the rebels. She didn't approve of Knox, naturally, because he attacked the absolute right of monarchs; he was an enemy of her class. But she was ready to use any power at hand to get rid of French influence in Scotland.

Mary of Guise died in 1560, with no close relative to sustain or comfort her. For days nobody dared break the news to Mary Stuart. When at last she was told, she was ill with grief. The Venetian ambassador said, "She loved her mother incredibly, much more than daughters usually do."

Fast on this calamity came another. François lay dying, six months after the death of Mary of Guise. It was probably a mastoid infection that killed him, for he had a terrible earache.

For forty days Mary mourned the young King's death

Mary's brief reign was over. She had been Queen for little more than a year; now at eighteen she was a widow. Her enemy Catherine was in power, acting as Regent for the boy King, François's brother. Mary gave the crown jewels to the new King and retired, as custom demanded, to a retreat of forty days locked up in her shuttered "dule chamber," wearing white mourning, and living by torch-light. She wrote a sad little poem to her husband's memory. It was sincere. She had loved him in a way; he had always adored her. She would miss him, but she would miss, far more, the position she had lost by his death. She thought of that as well as of François, while she sat in the mourning chamber.

CHAPTER THREE

The Widow in Scotland

IT MUST have been hard for Mary when she realized how far she had fallen—she who had held the most splendid position in Europe. She was now no longer Queen of France; Scotland was under English control, and her claim to being heir to the English crown was not recognized by anyone but her own supporters. She felt no love for her country, which she had nearly forgotten and whose people had treated her mother badly. It mattered nothing to her that Scotland was really beautiful. She was so

French in her outlook that she called it "her savage country": everyone at the elegant French Court spoke that way.

Yet it seemed that she would have to show more interest in that savage country, because she had no proper place anywhere else. Catherine de Medici was Regent in France, and she didn't want Mary around. The Guises, too, urged her to go to Scotland. They wanted to use her again in their always ambitious plans; they wanted to marry her to Don Carlos, the son of Philip of Spain. But Philip was cautious and said he was not at all sure Mary could make good her claim to Scotland. He pointed out that she had never actually reigned there. Would the Scottish Protestants let her return?

If the girl had not been genuinely brave she would have shrunk from the proof of this question. In Scotland, her informants said, John Knox ruled the roost. The grim-faced man had great influence over the people. He whipped them up to fever pitch when he preached. He minced no words, and constantly attacked the Catholic Church, until all the local priests were quite cowed.

Probably half the population, perhaps more, were still Catholic, but they were not the ones who ran things. The others, Knox's followers, were spoiling for a fight with Mary. They waited angrily to see what would happen when this Frenchwoman came to Scotland and tried to order them around. They had no intention of obeying a woman who attended Mass.

Mary could not simply arrive in Scotland, without making all sorts of arrangements first. Messengers and important officials went back and forth between Scotland and England and France. One of them was John Leslie, who wanted her to march into Scotland at the head of a Catholic army. He said that there were enough people on her side, if she rallied them, to drive out the Protestant leaders who formed the Congregation.

Mary refused to do this. She said the Queen must not make war on her subjects merely because they did not share her religious views. It would not be a matter of punishing treason, but of starting a civil war, which was different, and a wrong thing for a monarch to do.

However, this did not mean that she was on

the other side, that of the Reformists. Her brother James wanted her to join them, but she gave him the same reply. She must be on no side, she said. She wanted religious tolerance in Scotland. She would stay with her Church, and her subjects could stay with theirs.

Among other matters, her Secretary had to arrange for the passage. The waters of Britain were thronged with English ships, and things were in such a mixed-up state that it was not at all certain they wouldn't interfere with Mary's flotilla. So the Secretary asked Elizabeth to give Mary a safe-conduct, a promise that if the Queen of Scots was forced ashore on English soil she could pass through to her own country without hindrance. Otherwise, it was likely that Elizabeth would imprison her rival. More than one important Scot was already prisoner in England.

When this request was relayed to her, Elizabeth flew into a passion. The very name of Mary had this effect on the English Queen. For years she had been hearing of Mary—how charming she was, how beautiful, and what a strong claim she had to Elizabeth's throne. Elizabeth was jealous: she too was young, but she was not so young and pretty as Mary. However, this was not her only reason for hating the Queen of Scots. Elizabeth was a serious-minded monarch, very intelligent. She knew Mary might be a real danger.

Besides, Elizabeth was odd about some things, especially about the future. She could not bear to think or talk of her own death. She would not face the question, or discuss her possible successor.

This was a very inconvenient trait in a monarch. Henry VIII with all his faults had been a sensible king when he made his will, and thus avoided a bloody war for his subjects. In that one respect, his daughter was foolish. She was inconvenient in another way too—she hated to see other people get married, especially people near the throne, for marriage led to children, and each new child meant another possible rival. Elizabeth's courtiers knew they must keep flattering her. Whenever one of them married he fell from favor.

Mary wasn't a courtier and she had never flattered Elizabeth. In fact, she had sometimes said catty things about her cousin. These, of course, were always repeated to Elizabeth as fast as letters could carry the word from France to England. Proud Mary had said Elizabeth wasn't the legitimate heir, and that Anne Boleyn's family wasn't royal. When word reached Mary that Elizabeth was making a fool of herself about Lord Robert Dudley, the Queen of Scotland's comments were critical, though no doubt they were exaggerated by the time they were reported.

Worst of all, from Elizabeth's point of view, Mary had never signed the Treaty of Edinburgh which the English had composed. In this document, Mary was to promise that she and her husband would *never* claim the crown of England and Ireland.

So now Elizabeth declared that Mary could have a safe-conduct only if she would sign the Treaty first. Over in France this reply was taken in very bad part. Such inhospitality! Such bad manners! Mary said indignantly that if Elizabeth was going to be like that, she, Mary, would make the journey without any safe-conduct. If

She sailed from Calais in a lovely white galley

she was unlucky and had to land in England after all, then let Elizabeth do her worst. She might "do her pleasure and make sacrifice of me," said Mary. "Peradventure that casualty might be better for me than to live; in this matter let God's will be fulfilled."

Actually, when Elizabeth realized she couldn't get her Treaty signed by these methods, she relented and sent the safe-conduct. But it arrived after Mary's flotilla had gone.

The young Queen sailed from Calais on August 14, 1561. For a month there had been parties of farewell. Her ship was a lovely white galley; the whole fleet was a beautiful sight, for monarchs knew the value of pageantry. Torn with grief at parting from France, her girlhood home, Mary nevertheless was not completely wrapped in her own sensations. Always kind and thoughtful of her attendants, she gave orders that the galley-slaves who rowed her boat should on no account be whipped.

Standing offshore, the fleet waited for a wind, and Mary waited on deck, looking with all her heart and soul at the land she was leaving. Night fell. She had her couch made up on deck. At dawn the coast of France was still visible, a smudge in the distance which slowly sank out of sight.

"This is ended," said Mary, weeping. "Adieu, France. I think I shall never see you again."

At seven o'clock on August 19, when the fleet arrived at Leith, the port was dark and foggy and deserted. The royal party had arrived earlier than expected; the people who should have been there to do honor to the Queen were still in Edinburgh, three miles off. Word was sent immediately, but preparations took a long time, and Mary had to wait in the fog for some hours. All her party were dispirited and homesick for France.

John Knox, too, moaned about the fog, saying that Mary brought "sorrow, dolour, darkness and all impiety" with her. This was hardly fair of him; it usually *is* foggy in Scotland at that time of year.

It did not help matters that Mary's horses, sent on a separate ship, had been captured by the English. Local mounts had to be provided in a hurry, and they weren't very good specimens.

"Since I must change my Paradise for Hell, I must needs take patience," said Mary. It wasn't a tactful remark, but she must have been very tired.

At long last the welcoming committee straggled in and the Queen was transported in some sort of state to her palace of Holyrood near the capital. She had hoped to be able to move in with all her own furniture, which was much more valuable and elegant than the things her mother had left, but it had not arrived. She could not yet dazzle her Scots with the forty-five beds and thirty-six Turkey carpets and great tapestries and the best collection of jewels in all Europe; she had to depend on herself alone.

But her charm did not fail her. Even without these signs of wealth, Mary dazzled the suspicious nobles. Her sweetness and dignity and good manners had a wonderfully softening effect. The Lords of the Congregation were keyed up to hate the Catholics' ruler, but they swiftly changed their minds. They were proud of having a Queen like her.

For the first few days everything went much more smoothly than anyone had hoped. John Knox was confounded, and though he groaned and prophesied misery as usual, not many people listened. But then came Sunday, and Mary at Holyrood held her customary religious services. Word went round that the Queen was attending Mass.

This was too much for the extreme Reformists. As Knox said, "The hearts of the godly were pierced." A mob formed. Under the guidance of Lord Lindsay they stormed the palace, shouting threats against the Court priest. They might have hurt him, they might even have attacked Mary, had it not been for the Lord James. Although he was a Protestant, James did not approve of these methods; he was not a violent man. While Mary calmly went on with her worship, James guarded the chapel door.

Next day Mary and the Council issued a proclamation, so that such scenes might be avoided in future. It said nobody was to make any change in the religion that "Her Majesty found public and universally standing at Her Majesty's arrival." Nor was anyone to molest, for any cause, the people who had come from France. Everyone could follow his own religion but must not meddle with other people's.

This sounds fair enough, but John Knox was

not looking for fairness or tolerance: he wanted to stamp out the Catholics. In his next sermon he preached openly against the Mass. One Mass was more fearful to him, he said, than ten thousand armed enemies.

Because of this defiance of her proclamation, which had several unpleasant echoes, Mary sent for Knox so that she might reprimand him in person, and generally talk things over. She did not get very far with him, nor he with her; they were too far apart, the young Queen and the elderly fire-eater. Each spoke from his own prejudices and his own background and training.

Mary asked Knox how he could possibly claim to follow God's doctrine, yet teach the people to disobey their princes. God had commanded His subjects to obey their princes, she reminded him. Knox replied that religion came direct from God to the people, not by way of earthly princes, so subjects were not bound to frame their religion according to the princes' desires.

Mary recognized this as an attack on the absolute power of monarchy. To her, because she was Queen, this attack was treasonable. To

Knox, of course, it merely meant reform of a bad state of affairs. He had the deepest mistrust of kings.

"Think ye that subjects having power may resist their princes?" she asked, meaning in other words, "Do you really think you are right in standing up against me?"

Knox said, "If their princes exceed their bounds, Madam."

Mary might very well have asked who was to decide what these bounds were, but had she done so Knox would have replied without hesitation that *he* knew. He was always quite sure he was God's mouthpiece. When he got home he said, "If there be not in her a proud mind, a crafty wit, and an indurate heart against God and His truth, my judgment faileth me."

As the Court settled in and got used to Scotland, Mary's spirits rose, for she was young and resilient. She brought life and music and gaiety to Holyrood. The evenings were given to dancing and games. Everyone wore jewels and pretty clothes at Court. All this made Knox and his sour followers very angry. He thought dancing a devilish thing; he hated vanity and worldly beauty. His sermons grew more and more bitter. In roundabout ways he called Mary bad names.

Yet she lived up to her principles, and did not play favorites in regard to religion. When a Catholic clan, the Gordons, under their leader, the Earl of Huntly, stirred up a rebellion, she condemned it for what it was, and herself went out with her army to crush it. She loved the adventure; Mary always liked excitement and exercise and horses.

"I never saw her merrier," said the English ambassador. "She repented nothing but that she was not a man to lie all night in the fields or to walk the causeway with a Glasgow buckler and broadsword."

But she was not without misgivings. When the rebellion was crushed and Huntly dead, young Sir John Gordon was publicly executed as a traitor, and Mary had to watch. She fainted at the sight, and was carried out. People have since said that this was inconsistent in a woman who watched the tortures at Amboise without flinching, but it was not really inconsistent. She had been taught, all her life, that heretics deserved punishment. According to her training

Sir John was not a heretic; he was a Catholic like herself, and she must have felt a normal sympathy for him which she would not have allowed herself to feel for the wretched Huguenots.

However, little by little, Scotland did not seem so bad after all. Mary's brother James, now the Earl of Murray, was friendly and helpful, she thought. The plans for her Spanish marriage were still going on, and so she was sustained by the hope of once more attaining the splendid position her nature loved. She was cheered, too, at the prospect of living in a Catholic country where she would no longer feel like a prisoner. Catherine de Medici was opposed to the match and Philip of Spain would not give a definite answer, but still Mary hoped.

The rumor of the marriage grew loud enough to reach Knox's ears, and he preached against it. "All Papists are infidels," he declared.

This was too strong, Mary decided. Though their interviews never seemed to settle anything, she could not restrain herself in her indignation, and summoned him again. As soon as he appeared she began scolding him. Such

John Knox stood unmoved before the weeping Queen

was her anger that she wept as she talked. Knox replied calmly that he had to obey God's commands, and speak plainly when he was in the pulpit.

"But what have ye to do with my marriage?" she demanded.

He spoke about his duty to God and man.

"But what have ye to do with my marriage? Or what are ye within this Commonwealth?" the indignant Mary said.

"A subject, Madam," Knox replied. He went on to elaborate about his duty, and her nobles' duty, and the wrong it would be if the Queen were to marry an unbeliever. At last the infuriated girl again burst into a passion of tears. Knox just stood there, unmoved, while her attendant comforted and quieted her. As soon as she stopped crying he continued, "Madam . . . I never delighted in the weeping of any of God's creatures; yea, I can scarcely well abide the tears of my own boys whom my own hand corrects, much less can I rejoice in your Majesty's weeping. . . ." But he couldn't hurt his own conscience, he continued, or betray his Commonwealth through his silence.

Certainly he must have seemed a terrible and maddening old man. Mary tried to persuade the Lords to punish him, but they would not.

Suddenly Elizabeth veered round and became friendly. Warm protestations of affection passed by letter between the two women. Elizabeth showed a proper interest in her cousin's next marriage. She even touched on the awkward question of the succession, hinting that Mary might be Queen after her, if she married wisely. There were little jokes. If only Elizabeth had been a man, said Mary, they would have been able to marry each other and avoid all this trouble.

"I shall marry none but Elizabeth," she would say, laughing. She carried her cousin's letters, she declared, over her heart.

Visiting envoys between Edinburgh and London were much amused at the questions each royal lady asked about the other. Was Mary really so very pretty? Could she dance as well as herself? Elizabeth asked these questions urgently, and then showed off her own arts and graces like a jealous child. Mary in her turn asked eagerly about the color of Elizabeth's hair, and the state of the Queen's heart; what was the latest palace gossip about Robert Dudley?

Looking at the map, and at the closeness of the two cities, we wonder why the two women never met. But in those days monarchs rarely visited each other. Too many things were involved—pride and public opinion, and the risk of hostile demonstration or assassination. Yet Elizabeth and Mary did discuss a meeting, and planned for it. The encounter would have taken place if Continental war had not interfered. The meeting might have made a great difference to future events, but it was not to be.

There were several men Mary might possibly marry, and their names often came up in Elizabeth's council meetings. Not Don Carlos of Spain—the English wished to avoid any marriage that would join Mary with the ruler or near ruler of another country, just as they had wished to avoid her first marriage with the French Dauphin.

But there were men of English or Scots blood who had claim to a place in the English succession. There was the Earl of Arran for one, and there was Lord Darnley, the son of Lady Lennox, Mary's kinswoman. Lady Lennox, with Darnley, had long been detained in England because of Elizabeth's fear of rivals. However, it might be easier to dispose of them, reflected the

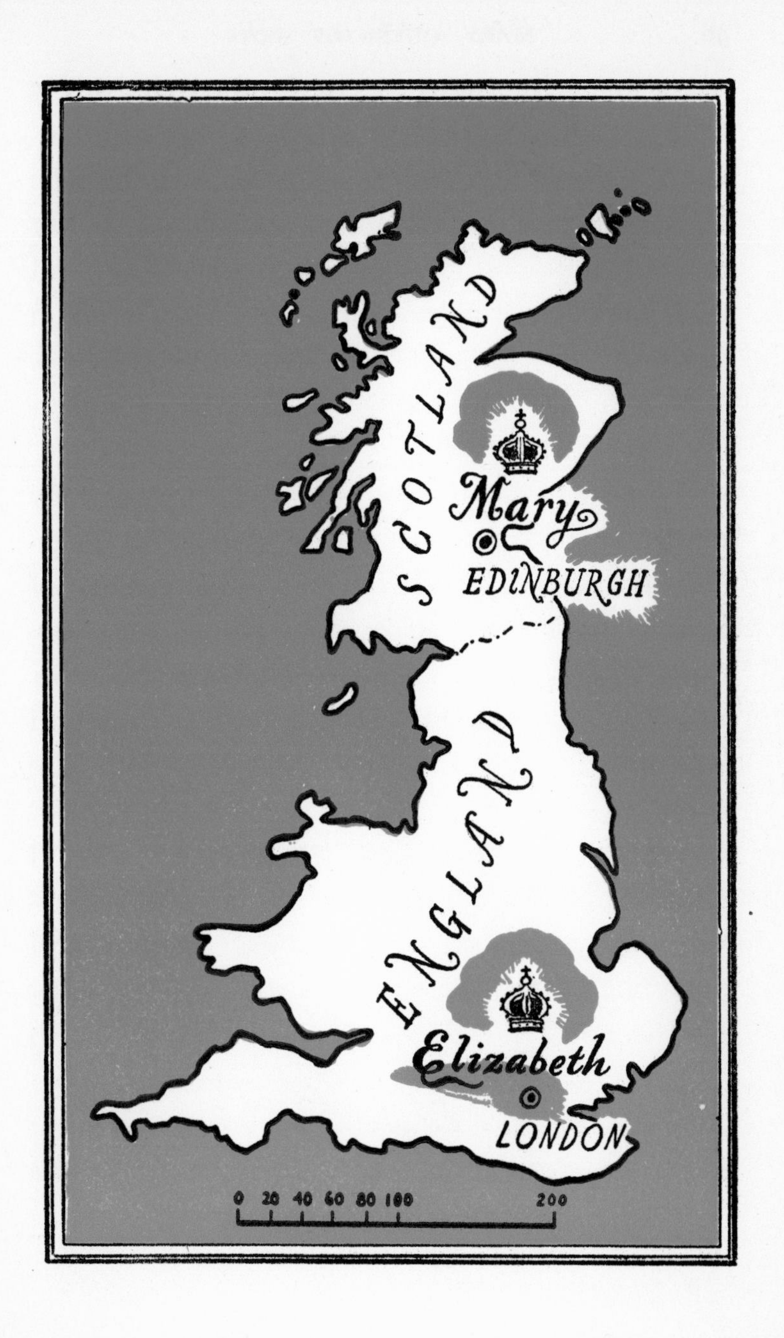
SCOTLAND
Mary
EDINBURGH
ENGLAND
Elizabeth
LONDON
0 20 40 60 80 100 200

English Queen, by giving them power and place in Scotland.

Unfortunately for the ladies' new friendship, Elizabeth suddenly sidetracked herself with another notion. Why, she asked, should Mary not marry Lord Robert Dudley, Elizabeth's favorite? Then the three of them could all live together happily.

Mary could hardly tell Elizabeth what she really thought of such a proposal. Queens didn't talk that way to each other unless they were at war. Mary had to go on pretending that she loved her cousin dearly, but in reality she was furious and felt she had been grossly insulted.

For two or three years, Elizabeth's fondness for Dudley had set all the Courts of Europe buzzing and whispering. When his wife Amy Robsart suddenly died, everyone said it was suicide, or perhaps even murder. His enemies asserted Dudley would have gone that far if he thought he had a chance of becoming King of England.

But Elizabeth never quite brought herself to marry Dudley. She may have loved him, but she loved her position better. She would not have shared her glory with anybody. And as long as she remained unmarried she could keep everyone guessing—Spain, France, the Holy Roman Empire, everyone in Europe waited and speculated and wondered whom she would marry. In England Elizabeth sat still, and kept them guessing, for she was clever. She knew that she held a valuable advantage as long as she wasn't committed to a man.

So, thought Mary, Dudley isn't good enough for Elizabeth, but he is quite good enough for me! If she thinks she can pass on her old lovers to me, she is badly mistaken.

CHAPTER FOUR

Darnley, Bridegroom and Traitor

IT WAS 1565 when young Henry Stuart, Lord Darnley, was permitted by Elizabeth to return to Scotland. He was not quite twenty-two, and Mary was twenty-three. For three years she had lived in her "savage country," and she was losing hope of ever being Queen of Spain. The dream, in dying, left an emptiness in her mind and heart. Perhaps it was because she was lonely that she liked Darnley as soon as she saw him.

As far as the boy's family was concerned he

would be a sensible choice as a husband. His mother was Queen Elizabeth's cousin and so a match would combine two possible heirs to England's crown. Elizabeth herself, thought Mary, could not refuse to admit the claims of any child of such a pair. And as for the stumbling block of religion, Darnley might suit both sides, for his mother Lady Lennox was a Catholic, yet he had embraced the Protestant faith. So the Scots would like him, and yet he might return secretly to the fold when once he was safely married.

But it was his appearance that most of all attracted the young Queen, with her sense of romance and her love of beauty. He was very tall, and this seemed good to a woman six feet in height. He was a rosy, blond boy, strong and athletic, and according to one observer, "beardless and baby-faced."

Mary and Darnley saw each other every day. At the house of the Earl of Murray, the name by which Mary's half-brother, James Stuart, was now known, Mary and Darnley had first met; there they often danced together. Mary declared he was "the lustiest and best proportioned long man she had seen." In spite of the dancing Darnley attended Knox's sermons sometimes. This made the Protestant Lords nod in approval.

Darnley was also fond of tennis, which he often played with Mary's private secretary David Rizzio, and a great friendship sprang up between the two men.

Rizzio was an Italian whom the Scots suspected of being a Papal spy, but Mary was fond of him. The two Continentals understood each other. She looked on him as an exile like herself from warmer, sunnier climes. Moreover, she needed someone in whom she could confide. It was becoming distressingly clear that Murray, her brother, was not to be trusted. So, in befriending Rizzio, Darnley did a clever thing, for the Italian used his influence to persuade the Queen to marry the young man.

Rizzio's chief argument was that Darnley was a good Catholic under his Protestant skin. The marriage would please the Pope. Mary found this sound reasoning. Besides, she reflected, by marrying Darnley she could flout Elizabeth as she had long wished to do.

Once again Knox insulted his monarch, and this time everyone agreed he had gone too far for his own good. It started again over the Mass. Mary was away at Stirling, but Mass was said at Holyrood anyway, by Catholic Scotsmen who lived at the palace. Angry Protestants, saying this was all wrong, forced their way into the chapel. Two of them were arrested and tried for violent invasion. Knox, to protect them, collected an enormous number of people and brought them to the trial. The show of force overawed the tribunal, and the men were released.

This was clearly an unlawful use of her subjects to prevent justice, said the Queen, and Knox must stand his trial for it. She was sure that she had him at last. Triumphantly she said, "Yon man gart me greit, and grat never tear himself; I will see if I can gar him greit." (That man made me cry and never shed a tear himself; I will see if I can make *him* cry.) But Knox's influence was too strong. In spite of all the Queen could do, he was acquitted.

The acquittal reminded Mary that after all she was among strangers whose point of view was hopelessly different from hers. More and more she listened to Rizzio and less and less to others. He urged her to marry Darnley. At last, while she was still wavering, the young Stuart caught the measles. Mary nursed him through the illness, and constant association did its work. She made up her mind.

Once she had decided, she was in a hurry to go through with the marriage. She had already written to Philip of Spain, asking what he thought of the idea, for Spain was an important Catholic power and Philip might start a war if he objected to the alliance. Philip did not object; he wrote warmly approving, and Mary took heart. Even a violent quarrel she had with her brother, the Earl of Murray, did not worry her, though he made dire threats of the consequences if she should marry Darnley. She sent word to Elizabeth, saying defiantly that she was determined on this marriage regardless of England's reaction.

It was necessary to get a Papal dispensation, that is, special permission to marry, as Darnley was her cousin. A request was sent for it, but Mary was in such a hurry that she didn't wait until the dispensation arrived. The marriage took place on July 29, 1565.

As a matter of fact, Elizabeth was not displeased. She may have hoped all along that this would happen, knowing Darnley was a weak antagonist. She refused help to her old friend Murray when he gathered some insurgents about him and rebelled against Mary. Murray had depended on help from Elizabeth, and when she let him down he was not able to put up resistance to Mary's soldiers.

The Queen's army went out after Murray under the leadership of James Hepburn, Earl of Bothwell. This Bothwell was of a type that stood out among the shifty Lords of Scotland. Though a Protestant, he was no follower of Knox, perhaps because Knox's family had been tenants of his people for more than a century. Bothwell had been loyal to Mary of Guise and he was loyal now to her daughter. He was a swaggering chip-on-the-shoulder fellow, an excellent soldier though rough in peacetime dealings. He had won a name for gallantry and recklessness.

Because of a brawl in which he had been in-

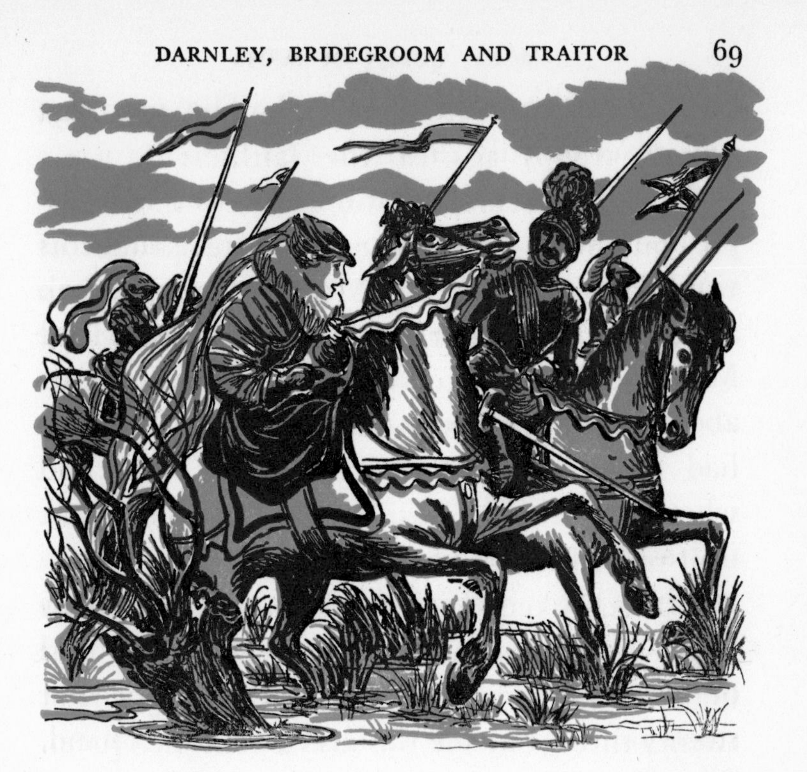

Mary rode with the troops against her brother

volved early in Mary's reign, he had been committed to prison in Edinburgh Castle. The facts were plain and Mary had no choice. However, she was not sorry to hear later that this loyal friend of her mother had made a daring escape, letting himself down from the rock on which his prison stood. He got away to France.

Pardoned, he returned just in time to lead Mary's troops against the faithless Murray. Mary herself joined in the chase; so did Darnley, but Mary was by far the better soldier of the newly-wedded pair. Murray was forced to flee across the border. He stayed in England for a time, sure that his easy-going sister would soon forgive him. This she did before the year was out.

If real life were like one of the Italian novels the Queen liked so much, she would have been happy until death with the man she loved. But her life was not a novel. She was a pretty girl of twenty-three, but she was also a genuine Queen with many worries. And her husband was not a fairy-tale prince. Far from it; he was a silly and unpleasant young man. Almost as soon as he had made the marriage which his mother and his own ambitious spirit wanted, he began to misbehave.

It was a bad case of swelled head. Too many people were ready to flatter and encourage Darnley. He drank heavily and picked quarrels with those persons who could have helped him.

Soon everyone was against him. He was so silly and unfeeling that he was rude to Mary herself.

Darnley was called King, but the mere title did not satisfy him. He wanted to be awarded the "Crown Matrimonial" by which he would have equal powers with his wife during her life. It would also empower him to rule after her death (as Mary of Guise had not been able to do when James V died). At first, if Mary had been able to do so without the approval of her Council, she might have given him this Crown and anything else he wanted. But when the Council held back, Darnley lost his temper about it and showed his unpleasant side, thus causing Mary to change her mind.

Any boy would have needed an extra strong nature to resist all the temptations the situation put in his way. Even an ordinarily good man might have resented the position, and Darnley was not that. He became positively ugly in his behavior. The bride and groom who had seemed so much in love in July were quarreling in December. Not long afterwards the King made a drunken scene at a dinner-party, and was so offensive to Mary that she left the room.

Yet she still showed some signs of fondness and compliance. The English ambassador reported that many people thought she had been bewitched, and he himself seemed to wonder. For in those days, everyone still believed in magic and love-potions.

One of the ways in which Darnley changed for the worse was in his attitude toward Rizzio. Darnley became furiously jealous of the man who had played tennis with him, eaten with him, and even slept with him. Mary preferred Rizzio to her own husband, he said. Why did she refuse to sit with the King in the evening? Why was she always sitting with Rizzio? Perhaps she loved the Italian!

This outrageous statement was obviously untrue, yet such remarks were bound to spread throughout the Court and make trouble for Mary. It was particularly scandalous because Mary was expecting a child. As she felt unwell, she was not able to defend herself as she would usually have done. And of course people leaped at the chance to repeat the ugly gossip. In the company of the great, there are always mouths to talk scandal and ears to listen.

David Rizzio too had developed a swelled head. Perhaps his success regarding the royal marriage was responsible, though for a long time before that his enemies had been ill-natured about him. They pointed out with truth that he was growing proud and dressing far above his station. He felt himself on top of the world. Since Murray had run away, the Protestant Lords were being careful and quiet. Rizzio said that Mary ought to push the Catholic faith further, as the Pope was always urging her to do. They had long talks about this. It was true that the Queen spent most of her time with him; Darnley's drinking had made him a bore, and David Rizzio was better company.

The more favor Mary showed to her Secretary, the more other people fawned on him and gave him presents. They complained about him but they paid, and he grew rich on it.

It was foolish of Mary to treat him so well, because she seems to have known that she was putting "Seigneur Davie" into danger by her kindness. It was not like her to be so clumsy, but there is an explanation. She was angry with Darnley, and disappointed. She was abnormally suspicious just then of almost everyone around her. Goodness knows she had reason to be suspicious every day of her life, but at this time, when she was expecting a child, she was not clear-headed. And so she turned to Rizzio, who was one person she was absolutely sure of, sympathetic to her in background and religion.

What people found most annoying was not Rizzio's love of wealth, for many courtiers had the same failing. They objected to the fact that he was a commoner, a base-born fellow who they felt had no right to live among them, wielding so much power.

Six months after Mary's marriage, a conspiracy got under way to do away with Rizzio. The moving spirits were the Lords Lindsay, Ruthven, and Morton, but Murray knew about it and did not interfere. Plans grew rapidly. First, it was necessary for the conspirators to get Darnley's help. They found it easy to persuade the angry, stupid boy to sign a bond with the others.

As time went on they planned to do much more than merely kill the Italian upstart. They would place Darnley on the throne and rule the land through him. They would stamp out the Catholic faith, and keep Mary in virtual imprisonment for the rest of her life.

For a conspiracy, this one was not very secret. Long before the climax, Cecil, the English Secretary of State, knew what was going to happen and told Queen Elizabeth. But neither she nor he gave Mary any warning, for they wanted her to come to grief. John Knox was another who was let in on the secret. He too thought it a good thing and waited eagerly to see it succeed, so that the Jezebel (as he called Mary) might be pushed off her pedestal and right-thinking Protestants rule in her stead.

On the night of March 9, 1566, Mary was at supper with Rizzio, the Countess of Argyll, and Arthur Erskine in a small room which led out of her bedroom in Holyrood. You can see it today, and go down the little winding stone staircase that leads to Darnley's bedchamber below. Suddenly the King appeared at the staircase door. Mary looked up in surprise, for it was not his custom to come in thus uninvited. Her sur-

Rizzio tried to hide behind the Queen's great skirt

prise changed to alarm when she saw Ruthven behind him, and caught the glint of candlelight on arms in the darkness of the stairs.

Rizzio understood too, and ran behind his mistress, but she could not save him. One ruffian jammed a pistol into her side to keep her quiet, and the others dragged the shrieking Rizzio into the bigger room. He clung frantically to the furniture while he was pulled along; he clung to the bedpost as he passed, and then the mantelpiece. They despatched him in an outer room. There were fifty-six stab wounds in his body when he died.

Through all this horror, the room where Mary remained against her will, clutched in Darnley's arms, was dimly lit by one candle which the Lady Argyll held aloft when the others were knocked over. Rizzio dead, the Lords returned, ready to continue with their *coup d'état.*

There was an excited scene, with Mary berating the assassins until Ruthven in anger declared that she had her own husband to thank for the crime. Mary put away this piece of information for later use. At the time, she realized she was in acute danger, so she mastered her temper and spoke calmly in order to protect herself and her unborn child. Her captors had no intention of allowing any communication with her ladies. Bothwell and Huntly, who were on guard in the palace, were locked in, but they managed to escape through a back window. Mary spent that night under heavy guard, a prisoner in her own house.

"No more tears now," she said. "I will think on a revenge."

Murray arrived next day, prudently late, as usual. At sight of her brother, Mary's affectionate nature overcame her caution. She fell into his arms, sobbing, "Had ye been here ye would not have allowed it!"

With tears in his eyes, James comforted her. Yet he had known all the time about the conspiracy. He planned to be the real King, getting rid of Darnley almost as soon as his sister was out of the way. Mary realized this from the way he greeted the conspirators, and she abandoned hope of his helping her. There must be another way out.

That evening, she declared that she was very ill and that a miscarriage was imminent. This seemed more than likely after all she had been through. Even the murderers dared not neglect her or risk her death, and so they allowed her ladies access to her. Through the ladies she got into touch with Bothwell, and they evolved a plan. It depended on her husband Darnley—Darnley the weak, the hopelessly unfaithful; Darnley who had brought this disaster on her.

Mary found it a simple matter to convince her husband that he would be better off if he helped her, instead of giving aid to the Lords. She reminded him of her powerful friends abroad. The turncoat turned yet again. That night when Mary escaped, Darnley went with her.

Everything was arranged in advance, and they crept out through a side door to where horses were waiting. Though the report of Mary's illness had been exaggerated, she was really not well, and dared not drive too fast. As they went on, Darnley, terrified of pursuit, constantly urged her to ride faster. When she pleaded that she could not, for fear of killing the child, he said,

"Never mind; we can have another!"

At this Mary lost her temper, and told him to go ahead and save himself. And that is what Darnley did—he actually rode far ahead of the Queen to save his own skin. At last she reached Dunbar in safety and there Bothwell's troops were waiting. But the memory of Darnley's sins remained with her. No woman could have forgiven such a man.

If she actually said that she would avenge Rizzio, as she was reported to have done, it should not surprise us. She must have said it several times in the course of those dreadful days.

Mary's ordeal had been a horrible one. The shock of the murder, followed by the threats of the brutal assassins and the fright she experienced for her baby, would have been enough to prostrate a weaker woman. Ordinarily, the Queen would have enjoyed the adventure of such an escape, but she was very near her time, and suffering from the knowledge that her husband was weak, vicious, and dangerous.

It was said in later years that James VI, her child who nearly met death before he drew breath in life, could not abide the sight of cold steel because of his mother's experiences that night. This is probably an old wives' tale, but of one thing we can be sure: iron had entered Mary's soul.

CHAPTER FIVE

An Heir to the Throne

"ADIEU, MADAM!" cried Darnley. "You shall not see my face for a long space."

But he never quite went away. He only said he would in order to frighten Mary, who knew what a scandal it would make if the King of Scotland left the country. Otherwise she would have been overjoyed to see the last of him.

The escape from Holyrood had knocked the bottom out of the rebellion. When the conspirators knew she had got away and was free to rouse the countryside against them, they ran for their lives. Darnley's father was among these frightened men; he hurried home to his estates. Most of the other leaders fled to England. Knox had a guilty conscience, and he left town too: this was a great triumph for the Queen. She was very popular when she rode into Edinburgh a week after the murder.

She wouldn't live in Holyrood because she thought it haunted. As soon as possible she had Rizzio's body reburied in the royal chapel. She put his younger brother into his place. Nobody dared to object, this time; not many wanted to. Elizabeth had one of her famous changes of heart when she heard the full story, and said that in Mary's place she would have stabbed Darnley with his own dagger.

Everybody felt the same way about Darnley. He floated about like a condemned soul, snubbed by his wife and everyone else. He had no friends at all now, for they knew he had betrayed both sides. He was a fool and would not accept the situation. He tried to force Mary to take him back into favor, but this she would not do.

Mary tried to keep up appearances, but more and more her good manners wore thin. She hated Darnley bitterly, and who could blame her? Though she forgave the other conspirators in time, and restored Murray to his former position near herself, she could not forget that Darnley had almost brought about the death of his own child.

The baby was born June 19, 1566—the future James VI of Scotland. He was also to become one day James I of England, the first Stuart to occupy the English throne. It was a happy time for Mary, and an unhappy one for her cousin in England. Word of the child's safe birth was brought to Elizabeth when she was dancing after supper. She stopped dancing, meditated for a moment, and burst out, "The Queen of Scotland hath a fair son, and I am but a barren stock!"

"The Queen and her husband agree after the old manner," reported the English ambassador, a month or so after little James's birth, "or rather worse."

A most important festival was pending in Edinburgh—the christening. But it was not due to take place until the baby was six months old, so that important officials from far-off countries would have time to get there. In the meantime, Mary took a short holiday in order to tone herself up: she went to Alloa, the castle of the Earl of Mar. A number of the Court went as well. Bothwell was there. He went almost everywhere now with the Queen. Mary was showing him more and more favor: to begin with, she was grateful to him, and as she grew to know him better she admired his strength and courage. Next to him, the whining Darnley made a worse showing than ever.

Soon Mary's partiality became the subject of gossip, just as it had done in Rizzio's day. People who did not like to see Bothwell getting so much power, spread scandal and said the Queen was in love with him. But this was not true—not yet, at any rate. Bothwell hadn't yet thought of aiming so high as to marry the Queen. How could he, when she had a husband and he a wife? He had just married Lady Jean

Gordon, the sister of his friend Huntly. Although Bothwell was supposed to be fickle and faithless, he really did seem to love Lady Jean.

The adventures of the Queen of Scots and her loyal lieutenant Bothwell now entered upon a new chapter. In October Mary was advised to make a journey to the south of Scotland, to Jedburgh, in order to hold an Assize. Too long had the rulers of Scotland neglected this region, where the clans waged fierce warfare against each other and acknowledged no master from the North.

It so happened that Bothwell's castle, the Hermitage, was about thirty miles from the town of Jedburgh. As Lieutenant of the Borders he went a few days ahead of the royal party, to round up lawbreakers and bring them in for trial. First he fought the Armstrongs, took prisoners, and locked them up in his castle. Then he went out against the Eliots.

During this battle Bothwell was wounded, and for several days his followers and Lady Jean feared for his life. When word was brought to Mary at Jedburgh, she was much concerned.

On the way back, her horse fell into a bog

As soon as the Assize was over she rode to the Hermitage to see how he was getting on. Finding him on the mend, she returned to Jedburgh, but during the ride her horse fell into a bog. The Queen was wet to the skin, and a dangerous illness—probably pneumonia—followed. She was so near death that for some minutes her ladies thought her gone. However, she had a good doctor, and she was a very strong woman: she pulled through.

Afterwards when people spoke about the tragedy that followed, they decided the mischief might have been done because of this illness, when Mary and Bothwell were both recovering at Jedburgh and saw each other every day.

The more Mary saw of Bothwell, the more she admired his strength and daring. They were qualities she liked above everything. As for Bothwell's feelings, he loved his wife, but he loved power more. Seeing that Mary was falling in love with him, he probably began to understand that it might be within his power to attain a crown.

Mary's illness had slowed up affairs of state, so the Privy Council met as soon as she recovered. The first matter they discussed was what to do about the tiresome Darnley, who was becoming a menace to everyone. Mary declared in agitation that unless she got rid of him somehow, she would never have a good day in her life, and everyone on the Council heartily agreed. But how was it to be done?

A divorce might be arranged, because of that Papal dispensation Mary hadn't waited for when she married. She could argue that the marriage hadn't been legal, and no doubt the authorities would grant the claim. But if Mary divorced Darnley, then people could say that her baby wasn't legitimate; it might spoil his chances of the crown. It was like the dispute over Mary Tudor. Mary would not hear of taking such a risk. So the divorce idea was dropped.

Another way out would be Darnley's death. The Lords Murray, Argyll, and Maitland were not too squeamish to discuss this possibility with Mary. There was the Holyrood rebellion; could they not accuse the King of treason for having taken part in it? During the murder he had held Mary in his arms against her will, to keep her from interfering: according to the strict laws that governed the persons of monarchs, this was treason. But the trial might be decided in Darnley's favor, and in any case they could not do anything yet, for the christening was to take place in a few weeks. A King's trial at such a moment would be embarrassing, to say the least.

Mary was in despair. Then Maitland, who had married Mary Fleming, one of the Queen's four Maries, said, "Madame, doubt yet not that we shall find the means by which your Majesty shall be quit of him, and that without prejudice to your son. And although my Lord Murray here present be little less scrupulous for a Protestant than your Grace is for a Papist, I am assured he will look through his fingers thereto."

This is a mystery story. Maitland's speech is a clue, and so we ought to examine it. It has two possible meanings. The first one to come to mind, of course, is that Maitland was slyly suggesting that Darnley be assassinated. But the other meaning makes more sense. The Privy Council, looking for ways and means, had thought of setting up a Catholic Court in Edinburgh. This Court would be empowered to discover some way to divorce the royal pair without putting the infant James's position in danger. Murray in the ordinary way would oppose any Catholic Court, but in this case he had evidently promised not to do so.

Mary said, "But I will have nothing done that may bring a spot on my honor or conscience."

"Madame, let us guide the matter among us,"

said Maitland. "Your Grace shall see nothing but good, and approved by Parliament."

And there the matter was left for the time being, and preparations for the christening went on.

CHAPTER SIX

Murder

THE BABY'S christening at Stirling Castle was magnificent. Queen Mary herself designed the suits of her chief Lords, and each was of a different color: Bothwell wore blue, Murray red, and Maitland green. She ordered a suit all of gold for the King, but alas, the tailor didn't have it ready in time for the christening on December 17. It didn't matter. Darnley refused to attend the party.

He was angry with the English ambassador, Lord Bedford. Bedford had brought Elizabeth's present, a beautiful font of solid gold, as well as definite instructions not to address Darnley as "King" or "Your Majesty." Elizabeth didn't want Darnley to get ideas about his own importance, now that a prince had been born. So when Darnley came into the room just as Bedford was paying his respects to the Queen, Bedford hastily retired. From that moment on, Darnley was not seen at the festivities.

He sulked in his own apartments, drinking. Outside, everyone was making merry. Only his attendants came near him, but they, too, were busy otherwise. The palace domestics even whisked off Darnley's own special silver dinner-service; it was needed for the great crowd at dinner. He had to eat off common pewter, and Darnley was a man who considered such things to be important.

There was a lot of talk about this state of affairs, as you can imagine. In public the Queen didn't give any sign that anything was wrong. But the French ambassador once came into her room unexpectedly and found her "laid on a bed and weeping sore."

People supposed it was Darnley she was crying about. They were beginning to think there might be some truth in the gossip that she liked Bothwell so much she would like to marry him. But poor Mary had many things to cry about, and she may have been upset about something else. For one thing, the new Pope was displeased with her. He was a man of very violent ideas, like her uncle the Cardinal. He thought she should have beheaded the conspirators of the Rizzio murder. He scolded her by letter for not doing this. He said she had fallen ill at Jedburgh because God was angry with her for being so weak and merciful.

She suspected, too, that Darnley was plotting to get control of baby James, throw her out, and set himself up as sovereign. Altogether Mary had plenty of reason to cry.

Still, she had plenty of reason to be happy as well. The baby was healthy, and she adored him. Her people were beginning to show that they liked her. And all the parties and pageants, fireworks and plays, dancing and jollity that went on for the week after the 17th were successful.

Queen Elizabeth sent a font of solid gold

It was Christmas Eve. Everything was over and the guests had gone, when Darnley suddenly made up his mind to go to Glasgow and stay with his father, Lord Lennox. It was not mere family sentiment that prompted him. He was in terror of his life, for he had just heard that the conspirators, pardoned by Mary, were coming back to Edinburgh. Darnley had a bad conscience. Knowing they would try to get revenge for his treachery, he ran away.

Just as he set out on the journey he began to feel queer. He rapidly grew so sick that he couldn't sit his horse without somebody to hold him up. He got to Glasgow by tremendous effort, and there went to bed. By this time he was covered with the dark spots of smallpox.

It wasn't a very severe case. We wonder how Mary felt when she first heard the news of Darnley's illness. She knew that he was mixed up in a plot to overthrow the throne and to put his own family, the Lennoxes, in power as Regents. Worse still, he had been corresponding with the Spanish, and had made a plan with them whereby the Lennoxes would help the Spanish conquer England and Scotland.

However, Darnley was recovering, so Mary must continue to behave in a wifely way, no matter how she felt in her heart. But she was not in a hurry to do so. She sent her doctor to Glasgow when she heard of the smallpox, but not for several weeks did she write to Darnley. At last, when he was on the road to health, she wrote and offered to visit him. She added that she and the Prince had moved to Holyrood.

Darnley was angry at her coldness. He snarled at the messenger and sent a nasty reply. He was sorry his castle wasn't the Hermitage, he said, and that he wasn't Bothwell lying ill. If he had been, he had no doubt Mary would be quickly with him.

Knowing it was no use paying attention to Darnley's spite, Mary made no reply. A few days later she went to Glasgow, as she had said she would do, but she probably wondered if the Lennoxes would strike while she was there. Darnley's servant waited for her four miles from town, with the welcoming committee, bringing the excuses of Lord Lennox. Lennox said he knew he had somehow offended the Queen and was afraid to face her.

"He would not be afraid were he not in fault," said Mary.

Naturally, she didn't want to stay at Lennox's castle. Everybody pretended to be very respectful, but the Queen never knew when rebellion might break out. Remembering Rizzio, she lodged in a house where she thought she might be safe. None of the important men of the city came to see her after she was installed. She knew this meant that they were on Darnley's side. If the Lennoxes did rebel, they would have help.

In those days it took plenty of courage to be a queen. You had to be ready for anything, all the time.

Mary's husband lay in bed and complained like a peevish child when she refused to live in his father's house. He said he wanted her to stay there so she could sit with him at night and nurse him and put his food into his mouth.

"I am young," he sniveled. Then he talked about the Rizzio affair and reminded Mary that she had never given him a formal pardon for it, as she had the others.

The Queen sat in the sick-chamber for two hours. Darnley said it was not long enough and wept as he complained. But she excused herself, saying his disease was still infectious. As Queen it was her duty not to take risks. The true reason was that she felt no love, tenderness, or pity for the man who had killed her faithful Davie, and who had nearly killed her child.

It was about the beginning of February, 1567, when the Queen brought her convalescent husband back to Edinburgh. He was still so weak that he lay on a horse-drawn litter, with a taffeta mask over his pock-marked face. There had been some discussion about where he was to go to finish his quarantine. He must not go to Holyrood because of baby James. Craigmillar, a large house of Mary's, had been suggested, but for some reason Darnley decided against that.

On the south side of Edinburgh just inside the city wall, there was a little house that might do. It was nearly in the country, in good air, and as it stood among a lot of gardens it was quiet enough for an invalid. The Canon of Holyrood, Robert Balfour, who owned it, offered it to Darnley. It formed part of the quadrangle of a ruined church called St. Mary in the Fields, so the district was known as Kirk o' Fields.

The house was very small, but like others in

Edinburgh it was strongly built of great stones, with walls ten feet thick in some places. Besides, it was connected to another newer house by a long hall, or *salle,* which could be used for Court gatherings, so the smallness of the house itself didn't matter. Both houses and the *salle* stood over a common arched cellar that ran their whole length.

All the necessary furniture had to be carried from Holyrood, but that wasn't much of a job. Beds, tapestries, chairs, and a few tables were enough. There were two storys: upstairs was the King's room and downstairs was the Queen's. The King's room had a balcony overhanging the city wall just where there was a gate.

Once the patient was installed, Mary had a busy time of it. First he had to be given a warm bath, a most unusual proceeding for the sixteenth century. It came under the heading of medical treatment. The Queen superintended this dangerous undertaking on the first day of Darnley's residence. Her plan was to spend half her time at Kirk o' Fields and the other half at

Holyrood. On the night of February fifth she slept at Kirk o' Fields, on the sixth at Holyrood, on the seventh back at Kirk o' Fields and so on. The ninth of February was a Sunday.

Sunday, like most days for Mary, was full of engagements. One of her waiting-women was married that morning, and Mary planned to give a dance for her that night at Holyrood. There was to be a state banquet at four o'clock and a state supper in the evening. At nine o'clock she would have time to drop in at Kirk o' Fields to visit Darnley, and she promised to do so, though she would have to return to Holyrood afterward to appear at the wedding dance. The shortness of her visit to Darnley would not matter. He had been declared fit to return to Holyrood on Monday.

It was a cold night and there had been a light snowfall. When Mary arrived at Kirk o' Fields, the larger part of her escort went to wait for her in the *salle,* but three men came with her to the sickroom—Bothwell, Argyll, and Huntly. We would think this was too much company for a sick man, but things were different in those days. Royalty seldom had any privacy, nor expected it. No doubt Darnley welcomed a little diversion after a dull day.

The men played a gambling game at a little table, shaking dice. Mary sat by the bed, chatting, and Darnley lay there in his taffeta mask, being pleasant-mannered for once. Two hours passed in this manner. Mary forgot to think of the time until nearly seven; then Bothwell's servant, a Frenchman named Paris, appeared at the door and reminded her that it was time to go home to the wedding party.

"Paris!" cried Mary. "How begrimed thou art!" In fact the man's face was very dirty, smudged all over with black sooty stuff. Mary stood up to go, and Darnley began to complain in his usual manner, like a child whose mother says good night. Just as a mother would, Mary laughed at him, and reminded him that the next night he would be home at Holyrood. Darnley seemed to be pleased. He had just written to his father that he was well and cheerful, and that the Queen was acting like "a natural and loving wife."

The Queen left with her escort. Darnley ordered his horses to be ready early in the morning for the move to Holyrood. He and his valet Taylor sang for a while, this being one of their customary amusements. Then after drinking some hot milk and wine, the King went to sleep. Taylor always slept in the room with him. Two other servants slept on the balcony.

There was confusion in the stories people told later of what happened then. Some said Mary had planned to go back to sleep at Kirk o' Fields. Then she changed her mind, after talking with Bothwell, who came to see her at the wedding party about midnight. According to these same people, Bothwell was accompanied by Traquair, leader of the foot soldiers. The men seemed to be arguing with the Queen, persuading her to something. Whether or not this story is true, she did not go back to Kirk o' Fields, but stayed at Holyrood.

At about two o'clock Edinburgh was awakened by a terrific explosion. The noise had come from the direction of Kirk o' Fields. Most of the citizens rushed there to find out what had happened. It was an amazing sight. The King's house and the long hall leading to the new house next door were gone. Only heaps of stone

Edinburgh was awakened by a terrific explosion

rubble were left of the whole solid edifice. Thick stone walls and arched cellars were all in ruins.

At first they could not find the King's body.

That was because they were looking where it should have been, among the stones. Finally someone stumbled across two bodies in the garden, a long way from the ruined house. One corpse was Darnley's; the other was Taylor's.

CHAPTER SEVEN

Dangerous Gossip and a Kidnapping

THERE WERE SOME very peculiar things about the King's death. In the first few minutes of discovery it was naturally thought that he and Taylor had been blown out of the house and into the garden by the explosion. But as soon as people had time to think and look around, they knew this would have been impossible. The bodies were a long way from the ruins; none of the rocks, even small fragments, had been hurled as far as that. There was a chair standing upright on the snowy ground near the pear tree beneath which the bodies were found, and a neatly folded dressing-gown of Darnley's lay by it. The chair might by some freak have been blown by the blast and still landed upright, but how could a dressing-gown remain folded after such an adventure?

Darnley wore only a nightshirt; Taylor a cap and one shoe. Now it was seen that the men had not been killed by any explosion. They had both been strangled, and a towel was still jammed into Taylor's mouth.

It was thought for a time that criminals had tried to murder not only the King, but the Queen too. An accident had saved Mary, the citizens told each other. For everyone had believed that she would go back to Kirk o' Fields to sleep that night. Luckily she had changed her mind and stayed at Holyrood. The wicked conspirators, clearly, had meant to blow up the whole Court party. They had put the gunpowder deep in the cellar, not only under Darnley's house but beneath the entire *salle*. Mary and her attendants had had a narrow escape.

When the Queen was told of the catastrophe she seemed as amazed and worried as anyone would expect. But she remained quiet and reserved long after the first shock. Her friends were surprised because they knew how she had hated Darnley. Some sign of relief would have been natural.

Lord Lennox didn't reply at all when Mary sent him word of his son's death. He didn't even ask for the body, so Darnley was buried without pomp, hurriedly, late at night in the royal chapel next to Rizzio's body.

After the funeral the talk began. Suspicion flourished. Who could have done it? People asked each other this question, and out of it grew uglier questions. After all, the Queen need not pretend that Darnley's loss was a grief to her. Was she worrying? People began to go over names in their minds, of those who would have wanted both Darnley and Mary dead, but there were not many.

Murray, the Queen's brother, might have. But Murray had gone out of Edinburgh two days before that Sunday night, and his absence seemed to free him from blame. It was possible, however, that he knew what was going to happen and had left the scene of the crime.

Lennox would not have wanted to kill his own son. Mary's friends would not have wanted to kill her. Perhaps—the thought struck several people at once—perhaps the murder was only *arranged* to look as if it had been aimed at her. Perhaps the assassins had wanted to blow up only Darnley. In that case, Mary must have been in on the conspiracy, and had stayed away on purpose that night.

But then why wasn't Darnley blown up? If he had been asleep in his room he could not have escaped.

Some clever persons figured out an answer to that last question. Darnley might have heard the noise of the powder being put into the cellar, or his men on the balcony might have heard or seen people sneaking through the little gate in the city wall with their loads of explosive. Warned by the servants, the King might have run out of doors to attack the intruders, though this did not sound like the kind of thing a coward like Darnley would do.

On the other hand, the King might have been just running away. Taylor probably ran after him like a good valet, carrying the warm dressing-gown his master had been in too much of a hurry to put on. Outside, the assassins caught the King and strangled him, and then killed Taylor so he wouldn't talk. That was the theory.

It was all very well, but it didn't explain the chair, and it didn't name the murderers.

Dismissing the problem of the chair, which has never been settled in all these hundreds of years, the gossips decided that the second problem—the murderers' identity—was all too easy to answer. Outside the palace group there had not been very much talk about Mary and Bothwell, but now everybody began to remember the bits and pieces they had heard.

Suppose there was something in it! Suppose Mary had asked Bothwell to get rid of the King? Perhaps she had asked Maitland and the others who talked it over that day when they had the conference. Perhaps Bothwell and Maitland and the others did it without letting her know.

Mary's enemies said she must have known. Her friends said she couldn't have known. Others who were Darnley's enemies (and that included an immense number of people) said it was some plot of Darnley's himself which went wrong. He must have gone out to meet his fellow-conspirators, they said, to wait with them in safety for a chance to blow up the Queen. Then there was a quarrel, perhaps, and he was killed. But he would hardly have gone out in his nightshirt, in that case.

What about Paris's dirty face that night? It was black with gunpowder, very likely. He must have been helping his master's men to bring the sacks of explosive into the cellar, while Mary and Bothwell were in the King's room. But would Mary have said anything about Paris's face if she had known why it was dirty?

The talk went on, around and around Edinburgh.

It spread beyond the city and the country. It reached the ears of Elizabeth, who wrote a troubled letter to her cousin. She said she thought Mary ought to know what people were saying: "that you have no desire to touch those who have done you such pleasure; as though the deed had not been committed without the murderers knowing they were safe." She begged Mary for her own sake as well as for justice's to punish the one who had done it, no matter who it might be.

Placards called "bills" appeared overnight, pinned on the doors of public buildings. It was a way the people had to spread word of anything they wanted to say without signing their names. Some of these bills said Bothwell had killed the King; some hinted at Mary herself.

There was a Board of Enquiry, but it did not settle anything. By this time the scandalous talk about Bothwell was so strong and loud that he could not pretend to ignore it any longer. He denied furiously that he had committed the crime. He said he would be glad to fight single-handed anyone who accused him of it. He said he would wash his hands in the blood of the bill-writers. But nobody admitted to having put up the placards.

Bothwell was one of the most reckless men in history. At this moment, just when public feeling was rising against him by the hour, he went calmly ahead and did something that asked for even more trouble. He arranged with his wife to get a divorce. Now everyone ever since Bothwell's marriage to Lady Jean had noted his fondness for her. If he wanted a divorce, it must be that he had strong hopes of a more ambitious marriage. There could be only one marriage that would tempt him so much that he would be willing to leave his wife.

Tongues raced, and now Lord Lennox broke his silence. He had kept quiet at first, because he was afraid that any investigation might disclose his rôle in a plot against the throne. But now, urged on by interested parties, he led the outcry against Bothwell. Genuinely grieving for his son, he printed and gave out copies of an extremely bad verse about Darnley's murderer, swearing that God would revenge "the slaughter of that innocent lamb."

At last, two months after the murder, the Queen bestirred herself and took the advice of Elizabeth and a dozen others. She hated to start proceedings because it would be dangerous, but they could no longer be avoided. In April the Earl of Bothwell was summoned with some of his underlings to stand trial for murder.

He was sure this would come to nothing, and he had good reason for this belief. We would open our eyes in wonder at sixteenth-century notions of justice. On the day of the Assize, Lennox marched up to Edinburgh from Linlithgow at the head of three thousand armed men. He claimed that they were merely his escort, that he was going peaceably to the trial to lay charges against Bothwell. But his trick did not work, for he was told at the city gates that he could bring only six of his men into town with him.

Wisely, Lennox refused to enter the city under such conditions. He knew that Bothwell had four thousand troops already entrenched there, ready to attack him if necessary. Without an army for protection, Lennox dared not appear at the Assize. He turned around and went home, and Bothwell for want of any accusing witness was acquitted.

Bothwell acted as if this acquittal were a complete clearing of his name. He paid no attention to sour looks and whispers. Instead, he swaggered about and repeated his challenge to his accusers: he would fight them in open battle any day they liked. It was all in keeping with his bluff character.

But Mary in the meantime grew even more

Bothwell forced each guest to sign the papers

quiet than she had been immediately after the funeral. What her thoughts were, nobody was sure, but we can guess that she was badly worried by all the criticism coming from England and France. Elizabeth might have taken some bold, resourceful action to stop people's mouths, but Mary was not tough enough. As a queen she had been brought up to think that whatever she did was right, but at the moment that faith must have been weakened. She felt forsaken by everyone but Bothwell.

A few days later Bothwell took his next step. He gave a big dinner-party to which he invited the most important nobles of the land. When everyone had drunk plenty of wine he brought out two papers and asked them to sign both. One was a promise to stand up for him against his enemies. The other was an agreement to his marriage with the Queen.

Taken by surprise and fuddled with drink, the guests did what their host wanted, but few of them meant it. Of course the proud Lords didn't want to see Bothwell saved from justice, and set up in a high position above themselves. Only Murray agreed to the bond with all his heart, and wrote to Mary advising her to accept Bothwell as a husband. The sooner she lost her throne on this man's account, the sooner would Murray get his chance.

Mary's story when she explained everything

was that Bothwell asked her to marry him on the day after the banquet, and she refused. She said she was surprised and angry; only his record of loyalty saved him from greater displeasure.

She went to Stirling the day after this conversation, to see the little Prince. Feeling against her was running so high that James's guardian, the Earl of Mar, would not let her take more than two ladies into the nursery with her; he was afraid she might kidnap her own baby and hand him over to Bothwell.

On April 23, 1567, Mary started back to Edinburgh. She broke her journey at Linlithgow, where she stayed the night. Bothwell and eight hundred of his men, that same night, were at Calder, between Linlithgow and Edinburgh near the Almond River. He was on guard with his men at the river in the early morning when the royal party arrived: Mary with Maitland, Huntly, Melville, and their attendants. Bothwell rode up and talked to Mary.

He said excitedly that there was a plot on foot to attack her party. She was in danger and must trust herself to him. They would foil the plot by going to Dunbar instead of Edinburgh.

The Queen may have believed the story and gone with him in good faith. It is like the story of the proposal—impossible to prove one way or the other. She sent a man to Edinburgh to give the alarm. Then without argument she turned and rode with Bothwell to Dunbar.

There the Queen stayed, or was held against her will, for ten days. If she told the truth, she had been tricked at first and then persuaded to consent to the marriage. If she did not tell the truth, her enemies were correct, and the abduction was all part of a plan.

Many voices were raised in her defense when it became known that she had signed a marriage contract with Bothwell, and that Bothwell's divorce from Lady Jean had gone through. It is odd that these voices were for the most part those of her enemies. Lennox said she had been given charms and potions. Catherine de Medici said she had been hypnotized. They seem to have agreed that Mary would not have married of her own free will. They were not really trying to excuse her, of course. They were attacking her new husband as the surest, quickest way to rob her of her crown.

Ten days after the kidnapping, Bothwell and the Queen came back to Holyrood. They did not come by way of the High Street, as Mary usually did, but by the less public Grassmarket Road. Bothwell was walking, leading Mary's horse. He was bareheaded and his men were unarmed. So they came quietly to the Palace, as if ashamed of themselves.

CHAPTER EIGHT

The Bothwell Marriage

AT A PUBLIC assembly of citizens, Mary said that she wanted to marry Bothwell, and was going to do so of her own free will. This statement was necessary to avoid riots against the man who had kidnapped the Queen, but it had a bad effect as far as Mary's popularity went. Thereafter, the people ignored her Secretary's story that she was an innocent victim. They resented the attempt to fool them, and were shocked that she should be willing to marry the man they believed to be her husband's assassin.

"God bless Your Grace if you are guiltless of the King's murder," a woman called after her in the street.

Not only the common people resented the marriage. Bothwell had more enemies than he could count among his peers. Elizabeth and the Kings of Spain and France were shocked because Bothwell had no blood claim to royal status.

The Catholic Church saw Mary slipping from their ranks. Bothwell insisted on a Protestant wedding, and that, they knew, was only the beginning. Especially did the Scots Catholics take alarm.

Only the very few true-blue faithful stuck to Mary at this time. Even they were prone to lecture her, or at least warn her. She knew that everyone was turning against her, but she would not listen.

On the night of May 14, the day before the wedding, somebody stuck up a bill on the palace gate, with a Latin line from Ovid: "The people say that only bad women marry in the month of May." Nevertheless, Mary was married next day. It was the quietest possible ceremony. According to custom the Queen wore mourning for Darnley. There were only a few guests. The French ambassador would not attend, because it was a Protestant ceremony. But he called on the newlywed couple afterwards, and found them anything but bright and gay. They had just quarreled, and Mary began to cry while she was talking and said she wished she were dead.

Through the days that followed she continued to be depressed and was often in tears. Once she was heard quarreling loudly with Bothwell, saying she wanted to kill herself.

Her ladies looked wise and said Mary was jealous of Lady Jean. They said she had found out what everyone else knew already, that Bothwell was still in love with his former wife. The men said Bothwell was jealous of Mary and treated her brutally. But we should not put too much confidence in this palace gossip, which was bound to spring up at such a time. Something worse than jealousy troubled Mary—fear.

She couldn't have failed to know that the

situation was desperate. A sovereign must be either strong or popular. For six years Mary had ruled Scotland without much strength, mainly by virtue of her personality. Now her personal influence was waning. She had no troops. Her only ally was Bothwell, the suspected murderer of her husband.

Bothwell's worries were less, but they were enough to make him bad-tempered with Mary. He was a practical man facing a grave emergency. He had reached the heights of ambition—or nearly: he was not yet King—but he was far from safe as yet. He had taken what he wanted; now he would have to fight for it.

Rebellion bubbled up on all sides, and the source of the boiling was Stirling Castle. Here Bothwell's enemies gathered around the cradle of Prince James. Nearly all the Lords of the land combined in an agreement to crown James king, appoint his Uncle Murray as Regent, and "set the Queen at liberty" from Bothwell. Maitland quit his recently acquired post as Mary's Secretary two weeks after the wedding, and joined the rebels. Balfour, who was in charge at

Mary disguised herself as a page and slipped away with Bothwell

Edinburgh Castle, was with them in spirit, though Bothwell did not know it. Everybody, in fact, but the hard core of Mary's loyal followers, had gone over to the other side.

Less than a month after the marriage a rebellion broke out. The Queen called on her lieges to meet her, and then she and Bothwell hurried to Borthwick Castle in the South, just as the rebels moved into Edinburgh. Rebel troops followed the royal pair to Borthwick and surrounded it. Bothwell slipped out of the Castle in disguise. When the mob discovered this, most of them retired. Mary disguised herself as a page. She slipped safely through the few lines still drawn up around the Castle and met Bothwell outside. The two then rode in great haste to the safe walls of Dunbar.

For all the danger of the situation, it was the kind of adventure Mary liked. Perhaps this one night, galloping through the country, was the happiest time she experienced during her tragically short marriage.

On the 15th of June, a month to the day after her wedding, the couple faced the enemy. They were as ready as they would ever be. They could not muster as many as three thousand men, for Mary's soldiers, like the rest of the Scots, did not relish obeying Bothwell and many had deserted. Such as the army was, they led it out of Dunbar Castle to Carberry Hill.

Mary, who had escaped from Borthwick without any of her clothes, was dressed in an ordinary and rather poor costume borrowed from a soldier's wife. It was made up of a short red petticoat, velvet hat, and sleeves tied with "points," that is, ribbons with metal tags. Never before had this lovely woman appeared in anything but the splendid robes of a queen.

The army of the enemy stood at attention, ready for battle. Mary's troops were in much less warlike mood. Before anyone began to fight, the Lords sent a message to the Queen through du Croc, the French ambassador, offering terms. They had two suggestions. Mary must give up Bothwell and come to them; they would then serve her with all their former allegiance. Or Bothwell could fight it out with one of their warriors.

Mary refused flatly to leave Bothwell. As for the single-combat idea, she would not permit it. Bothwell told du Croc to stand by for all-out battle. He was quite ready for it.

Unfortunately, his army was not. When he gave the order to advance, the independent

Scots insisted upon more talk instead. All this waiting about in the open, looking at the much bigger army against them, had weakened the men's spirit for the fight. Many of them had run away since morning.

Night was now drawing on, and Mary's fears increased. Bothwell must escape, she said. Let him run for his life, and when she could get free of all her entanglements they would meet again.

It was a heroic decision, worthy of the daughter of Mary of Guise. She had been cowardly when it came to letting him fight, but now she was brave again. To save her husband she had refused to disown him. Now, without disowning him, still wishing to save him, she sent him away.

Their farewell convinced everyone that the Queen had indeed married Bothwell of her own will and for love. "She caused the duke to depart in great pain and anguish," wrote a soldier who witnessed the scene, "and with many long kisses they took farewell, and at last he asked her if she would keep the faith she had given him and she answered that she would. Thereupon she gave him her hand and he with a small company galloped off to Dunbar." Then Queen Mary turned to face whatever might be in store for her.

CHAPTER NINE

The Casket Letters. Escape

MARY WOULD have been foolish to believe all the fair promises the Lords made when they urged her to surrender. Not having believed them, she felt no surprise upon finding herself a prisoner in their hands, but she was furious. Her beloved husband had been torn from her. That was the worst of the rebellion. But it seemed infuriating and shocking to Mary that the rebellion was taking place at all. She scolded and raged at the nobles. Now and then she wept from anger and exhaustion. Now and then she collected herself and took hope, looking eagerly into the distance for the reinforcements she thought Bothwell might be bringing to her aid.

They took her back to Edinburgh in ragged procession, led by their special banner. On this banner was a picture of Darnley, lying dead and naked under the pear tree, and a new-born baby, supposed to be Prince James, looking down on the body. Coming from the child's mouth were the words, "Judge and avenge my cause, O Lord."

The streets of Edinburgh were choked with contemptuous and angry people who crowded to see the captive Queen. It was bad enough for poor Mary to be seen in a red petticoat with her face dirty and tear-streaked, but the jeers and shouts brought on one of her fainting spells. She was hurried into a house in High Street and locked alone in a little room; there under heavy guard she spent the night. By morning she was hysterical. With her clothes half torn off, she shouted from her window, appealing to her people either to kill or release her.

But during the course of the day she took heart, and was strong enough to resist all the

Mary appeals to her people either to kill or release her

efforts of her captors when they tried to treat with her. They urged her to declare her marriage void. Mary said no; she was with child and would not ruin that child's name. They wanted her then to swear that Bothwell had murdered Darnley, and to send out a royal decree to have him brought in and punished. Mary retorted that if Bothwell was guilty, so then were most of the Lords themselves.

Of course this was true. In a final effort to bring the Queen around to what they wanted, the Lords went to work on her jealousy. They told her that Bothwell had never loved her; that he still considered Lady Jean his true wife.

It was all of no use. "Though her body be restrained," one of them reported to Cecil in England, "yet her heart is not dismayed."

"Put me on a ship with him, my husband, and let us go where fortune wills," said Mary.

No doubt the nobles would have done this cheerfully enough, if they could have been sure she wouldn't come back later with an army behind her, furnished by France or Spain. But they knew she was a fighter. Some of them were gravely worried by the turn they thought events were taking. In spite of the feeling they had whipped up, there was some sympathy for Mary among the public. And the nobles knew Elizabeth was not likely to approve this sudden upsetting of a throne.

That evening the Queen was taken back to Holyrood, still with the guard, the ugly Darnley banner flying ahead of them. She thought she was to remain at Holyrood, and she grew hopeful again. Two of her Maries met her, shedding sympathetic tears at her plight. They managed to supply a nightgown, though Mary's own possessions had all been looted.

But she had scarcely begun to eat her evening meal when an order came; she must prepare for another move. As she had no wardrobe left, the preparation was sketchy. She dressed in a short gray garment. A broken-down horse was given to her—"a carrion jade found by chance in a pasture."

The traitors, not therewith content,
Did lead her thence away,
And changed all her brave attire
Into a frock of gray.

Mary had supposed she was being taken to her child. Instead she found herself imprisoned in the castle which stands on the island of Loch Leven, under the care of Lady Douglas, Murray's mother. Although Margaret Douglas was not unkind, and the conditions under which the Queen was to live were fairly luxurious, nothing could make her feel better about her misfortunes. To add to her woes, ill health again overtook her.

The Lords reasoned with her as she lay in bed. They kept urging her to forswear Bothwell. Steadfastly she refused. She wrote to her husband to tell him that she would not forsake him, but the message was intercepted.

Then her enemies got hold of the now famous Casket Letters.

These papers were exactly what her enemies needed to put themselves in the right with Mary's adherents and friends. They were so useful that many pro-Mary scholars have decided that they were improved, if not invented, by the Lords themselves.

The Casket was a small silver-gilt chest, or coffer, that belonged to Bothwell. His servant had taken it from the palace and hidden it in a house in town. When the Lords captured the man and tortured him, trying to find out whatever they could against Bothwell, he confessed to having this box and surrendered it to his tormenters.

Damaging letters were found in the silver-gilt Casket

Inside, it was later claimed, a number of love-letters and sonnets written by Mary were found. The Lords produced copies of these documents to prove that the Queen had been mixed up in Darnley's murder; that she and Bothwell had been accomplices.

If the letters are genuine, there can be no doubt that Mary was as guilty as her enemies said she was. But the Queen's champions have produced arguments in her favor, and their points are worth attention.

The most interesting fact is that no one who might be inclined to favor Mary ever saw the original papers. Nobody whose word was disinterested ever saw them. Only her accusers claimed to have handled the letters and recognized the writing. This is significant, because it leaves the possibility that they were either forgeries or real letters that were tampered with, altered, and added to. Such tricks are not unknown when rival parties struggle for power.

It is also a good guess that the poems in the Casket were not written by Mary. They are not at all her style, and the French in which they are composed is faulty. Hers would not have been.

It seems likely that the poems were written by a Danish lady named Anna Trondsson, whom Bothwell had met during his exile on the Continent. He treated her very badly, for though they went through a marriage ceremony, he later walked out on her. He did worse: he took all her fortune with him and refused to send it back.

As for the prose letters that caused all the excitement, though most of them might quite well have been written by Mary, there were passages which were not at all in character. That is why a good many people think they were cut and altered to look as bad as possible.

Elizabeth gave her cousin the benefit of the doubt and said she would not believe in Mary's guilt. But the nobles had Knox on their side. He preached that Mary "hath no more liberty nor privilege to commit murder or adultery than any other private person, either by God's laws or the laws of the realm." The excitement caused by these republican sentiments made his listeners forget to question if the Queen had indeed committed such crimes. They began to demand a public trial, royal blood or no royal blood.

But the Lords did not want a public trial; they had too much to conceal about their own part in the crime. Instead, they turned their efforts to persuading the Queen to abdicate in favor of the little Prince.

Mary fought for a long time and would not hear of it. But some secretly friendly nobles assured her that any bond she signed under duress would not hold good when it came to the test. There was no doubt that she was under duress. Not only was she imprisoned, but her captors threatened her with dire hints as to what would happen if she did not sign away her crown. They meant it. Some of them were willing and eager to put her to death, and Mary was certain that they would try to poison her.

From England Elizabeth sent a strong message that her cousin must be set free. However, her ambassador had to report that the more the English Queen threatened, the more likely it seemed that the reckless Scots nobles would kill Mary.

At last, some time in July, 1567, Mary signed the abdication paper. It was a strange, intense scene. Lord Lindsay gripped her arm to force her to take the pen, and after she had written her name she showed everyone in the room how he had bruised her. The Queen was sure the time would come when she could call these people to account. Her whole life and hope were bound up now in that longed-for day. She had miscarried Bothwell's child, and had only herself to think of, now that Bothwell had escaped.

For the present the Lords triumphed. They had Mary's abdication, signed and sealed. Little Prince James was crowned at Stirling that same month, nearly as small a sovereign as his mother had been at her coronation twenty-five years before. For Regent, Murray was chosen. That clever man had been away from Edinburgh, as usual, while all the active trouble was going on. Now that things were quiet he came back, but he was in a bad temper; he had discussed the matter with Elizabeth and she had flatly refused to support the abdication. Mary must be freed, she insisted.

Murray went straight to his mother's castle to visit Mary. This time he showed himself in his true colors, and lectured her severely for all her misdeeds, as he called them. It was not in his power, he said, to help her to get out.

The Lords were confident that they had put

Disguised as a laundress, Mary attempts escape but her identity is discovered by the boatmen

their prisoner in a safe spot. Not only was she in a strong castle, but the castle itself was on an island. They had yet to discover how resourceful the Queen could be, and how great was her appeal for romantic young people.

Margaret Douglas's younger son George, living near Mary all through the long winter, fell in love with her. Before the spring of 1568 she and Geordie had evolved a plan for her escape. It was simple enough. One April day a laundress came from Kinross as she did every week to fetch the dirty clothes, being rowed over to the island in a small boat. She was easily bribed to let Mary change clothes with her and take her place in the boat on its return journey.

The trick was almost a success. Mary, with her face muffled up, was halfway to shore when one of the boatman jokingly said, "Let's see what she looks like." The Queen put up her hands to shield her face. The boatmen noticed that the hands were white and well cared for, as a washerwoman's could never be, and they were frightened. They turned around and brought poor Mary back to the castle.

For this escapade Murray made his mother

banish Geordie Douglas from Loch Leven. But on the mainland in Kinross, the young man went on plotting to get the Queen away. He had an accomplice in the castle, a kinsman known as Little Douglas. One night Little Douglas stole the keys, let Mary out, and locked the garrison in. He scuttled all the boats but one, and in this she escaped.

Mary's faithful follower Lord Seaton was waiting on shore with a good horse for her. By the time the alarm had been sounded and shots were ringing out, the Queen was landing at a prearranged spot. She rode nearly twenty miles, and by midnight was safe—temporarily—at Niddrie Castle. Great was the rejoicing among her friends.

In the midst of all the happiness and excitement of her escape, Mary of course thought of Bothwell. She tried to get in touch with him, but she could not. Bothwell had been overtaken by a grim fate. After he got away at Carberry Hill, he never managed to collect enough followers to make a stand against his pursuers, let alone lead a rescue party for the Queen.

After one or two disastrous battles, he fled from Scotland, crossed the North Sea, and arrived at Bergen in Norway. He could not have chosen a worse place as a refuge. The governor of the castle there was the brother of Anna Trondssön, the lady Bothwell had deserted, and whose fortune he had stolen. The fugitive was immediately clapped into jail. There we may as well leave him, for he was never to get out again. Years later he died, raving mad, in irons.

CHAPTER TEN

Defeat; the Long Years

SIX THOUSAND MEN had been mustered under Mary's loyal Lords. Unfortunately for her cause, her friends had not the military talent to match their staunch hearts. Murray was sure of himself now, and he did not bother to pretend any more that he was on her side. As Regent he collected a large number of troops and sent them out to capture the Queen. They intercepted her forces at Langside near Glasgow, as the latter were marching towards Dumbarton.

Mary and the faithful Mary Seaton watched

the battle of Langside from a hill half a mile away. It must have been a heartbreaking sight, for the Queen's men had no chance at all. The Regent's forces out-guessed and out-fought them in less than an hour, and those Queen's men who were not taken prisoner broke ranks and fled.

Nothing was left for Mary then but to run for her life. She was so near the victorious troops that there was no way to get past them to Dumbarton. Instead, with Mary Seaton and five men (the young Douglases among them), she made for the Solway Estuary, which cuts deep into the coast between England and Scotland. She and Mary Seaton separated for most of the journey. Mary Seaton dressed herself as the Queen so that their pursuers would be led astray and follow her, but neither woman was caught.

Still, it was a very near thing. The Queen could not reveal herself to anyone they met on the way, for fear some peasant would betray them. Once, in a deep lane, she was nearly cut down by farm-workers scything their grain.

"For twenty hours the Queen was without food and drink, and endured famine, cold, heat,

The Queen embarked for England on a fishing smack

and flight, not knowing whither, riding ninety-two miles across the country without stopping or alighting. She slept upon the ground, and ate oatmeal without bread, and was three nights like the owls, without a female to aid her."

The battle of Langside was fought on May 13. On the 16th the Queen got to the coast of the Solway, near Dundrennan, at a place now called Port Mary, and there embarked on a fishing smack. Scotland was left behind.

It was her plan to go straight to England, only a few miles across the water, and take refuge with Elizabeth. A few months before, she would never have dared to do this. In spite of all the friendly letters which had passed between the women, the Queen of Scots knew that Elizabeth should not hold her cousin's fate in her hands. But there was not much choice now, and Elizabeth's latest acts had been so helpful and reassuring that Mary changed her mind. To go merely to England seemed much safer than attempting the long way around by sea to France.

Lords Herries, Fleming, and Livingstone, who with the Douglases made up her escort, advised strongly against England. At all costs Mary must try to get to France, they said. Herries even went down on his knees and begged her not to trust Elizabeth. His counsel had effect, and when the fishing smack was halfway across the estuary, Mary decided to go to France after all. However, it was too late to change course now, especially in that frail vessel. The wind carried them to Workington on the coast of Cumberland, which is England's northernmost county.

Mary was at last in Elizabeth's country. Almost her first act was to send off word to the Queen, her cousin, asking to be received at Court. "For I am in a piteous condition not merely for a queen but for a simple gentlewoman. For I possess nothing in the world but what I stand up in."

Elizabeth was in an awkward corner. She had never expected her warm sympathy to have quite such a definite result as this. There was Mary, and there were all her own promises. What was she to do?

First, knowing what the world expected of her, she thought of inviting her cousin to come right away to London and live with her at Court. Then second thoughts interfered, as they usually did. Mary would not be easy to handle. The Catholics of England were difficult enough to manage as it was, and if Elizabeth showed such encouragement to their heroine, who knew what might happen?

There were various anti-Mary kings to think of, and their opinions. Also, what of Scotland? Elizabeth had been encouraging Murray, off and on, for a long time; did she really want to get embroiled with those Lords now in power across the border? She did not. Elizabeth never wanted war with anyone: she knew what it would cost.

Even now, up north in Carlisle, Mary was making trouble. What might not happen in London, if she came? It was not her fault, but she was a young Queen, and that in itself spelled trouble. In the minds of men, the possession of a woman like Mary in marriage was better than gold or jewels. It meant power. Whenever men came into contact with Mary, ambition set to work in their minds. They always began to think, "How can I marry her?" or at least, "How can my nearest relation marry her?"

This ambition sprang up in Mary's footsteps as soon as she stood on English soil. The country gentry among whom she found refuge were Catholics. They hurried to see the romantic Queen of Scots, their breasts burning with hope for their religion and their own futures. Mary was under watchful guard—by order from London—but she held court all day with her visitors nevertheless. They were utterly charmed with her.

Elizabeth made her decision, and replied coldly. She regretted, she said, that she couldn't receive Mary until Mary had cleared herself of the rumors that she had anything to do with Darnley's murder. The man who brought the message, Sir Francis Knollys, was placed in the position of being the keeper of Mary. The Queen of Scots had become a ward, or prisoner, of Elizabeth.

In this state she was to remain for the nineteen years of life that were left to her.

At first, Mary did not despair. She never did despair. She was a courageous woman, and all her time was spent in attempting, one way and another, to get out of Elizabeth's hands. The only time Mary wasn't planning, or writing letters, or doing both, she was ill.

When Knollys was taking care of her he was much impressed by her qualities. He wrote in his reports that the Queen had "an eloquent tongue, a discreet head, a stout courage and a liberal heart. . . . Surely this princess is a notable woman!" "She delights to hear of hardiness and valour," he wrote again, "commending all approved hardy men of her country, even though they be among her enemies, and not concealing cowardice of friends. . . . And surely she is a rare woman, for as no flattery can lightly abuse her, so no plain speech cometh to offend her if she think the speaker thereof an honest man; and by this means I would make you believe, she thinks me an honest man!"

Mary had by this time realized that Elizabeth would not help her to regain her throne; worse, she knew she must remain where she was, or anywhere Elizabeth might decide. The great disappointment was heralded by a small one. Because Mary had asked for clothes, Elizabeth sent her a parcel containing miserable rags—two torn shifts, two worn pairs of shoes, and two scraps of velvet. The Queen of Scots, always generous herself, was shocked and scornful of such meanness. Fortunately, Murray after a time restored Mary's own clothes, though he didn't return her jewels. Of these he kept the greater part. He sent one magnificent string of Mary's pearls, however, to Elizabeth!

At the end of June the English Queen decreed that an inquiry should be held to decide between Mary's protests of innocence regarding Darnley's murder and Murray's declarations that as she was a criminal, he had been right in deposing her. Mary was warmly indignant that anyone should dare put a Queen on trial. But she would allow Elizabeth to judge, she said, if she would have a personal interview with Mary first.

Of course it was not in Mary's power to set such conditions, and she didn't get her way. Elizabeth finally produced other terms which Herries, as Mary's ambassador, accepted. If the rebel Scots Lords could not prove to the Commission that they had been justified, Elizabeth said, Mary would be restored to her throne, by force of arms if necessary.

The Commission met in York in October. It was impossible that they should arrive at an honest decision, there were so many intrigues and counter-plots. For example, Maitland could not speak out as he might have wished to do, because he knew Mary had Bothwell's list of accomplices and their signatures, including his.

On the other hand, Mary was not allowed to attend the hearings. The Casket Letters were produced and their contents shocked everyone grievously, but it was pointed out in Mary's defense that they were merely copies. Nobody produced the originals. The Casket was merely one more doubt to add to the others.

The Commission was transferred to Westminster before it was all done with, and the final result was inconclusive. The only thing definitely decided was that Mary wasn't cleared to such an extent that Elizabeth could receive her at Court.

The following years of Mary's life appear to go in a kind of irregular pattern of waves. There are a good many little waves, representing the times that Elizabeth "investigated" the case, suggesting this or that agreement by which, she said, Mary might be set free. Each time, the poor prisoner became happy and excited, only to have her hopes dashed. There are a few stretches when nothing happened; these occur more often toward the end. Here and there are high waves, when Mary's hopes rose dazzlingly high, and some of her endless plotting seemed to be bearing fruit.

The waves of Elizabeth's making were not sheer cruelty, or moves in a cat-and-mouse game. Some historians have thought they were, and have bitterly blamed Elizabeth for her brutal treatment of a cousin and a queen. But in their love for Mary these men have forgotten that Elizabeth did nothing from mere idle cruelty. She was first, last and always a statesman. She didn't always do the wisest things: she often made mistakes in policy, but she never stopped thinking of her duty as Queen. Whatever treatment she gave Mary, even the final tragedy, was always because of some hope that she might gain a point. She was cruel, but not wantonly so.

Just like everyone else, sometimes she thought of marrying off Mary and profiting from the match. In the affair of the Duke of Norfolk, she pretended when it was disclosed to be shocked and surprised, but she had known something of the plan for a long time and had for a while approved of it. It is a strange story.

Norfolk never met Mary, yet for a long time

he tried earnestly to marry her. Mary never met him, but she accepted the idea eagerly, and wrote letters to him declaring that she loved him dearly. Norfolk hoped by marrying Mary to become King of England, and from this hope he was led into a conspiracy against the Crown. He agreed to aid the King of Spain by overthrowing Elizabeth. Mary, for her part, hoped by marrying Norfolk to be set free and to occupy a throne once more.

However, the plot was exposed. Norfolk was condemned and executed for treason. Thus he died for the sake of a woman he never saw.

The English Court wondered if Mary was not in fact some kind of sorceress, since men were so ready to risk the gravest dangers for her sake. They redoubled their guards, for fear she might bewitch more young men and make her escape as she had done before.

Two or three times the worrisome ward was moved about. A year or so after her ill-fated arrival, the Catholic Lords of the north of England rose against Elizabeth, spurred on no doubt by the near presence of the romantic Queen of

Scots. The rebellion was put down, and Mary was prudently taken farther south where she would not be a perpetual inspiration to her friends.

Week succeeded week, month came after month. She was not treated as an ordinary prisoner. She lived in luxury of a sort, and whenever Elizabeth's scanty allowance ran short, Mary's own money made up the difference for herself and her attendants. She had her little outings, carefully guarded; she had her needlework and a few friends. But she was a prisoner for all that. Her queenly spirit suffered sadly.

Hope kept her going through the years. In all that time she never stopped conspiring. Letters poured out of the great country houses where she was held; they had to be smuggled out, but there was always someone to help. Letters flowed out and in, sometimes in the hands of her attendants, sometimes by means of bribed servants, most often in the ever-useful laundry-basket. In the course of the years Mary spent most of her fortune in this manner.

Important news usually came to her ears,

even when she was not officially informed. She heard of Murray's assassination, in 1570, and she was so frankly overjoyed that she settled money on the assassin. But there was never fresh news of Bothwell, and she didn't ask about him any more.

The years went by, until Elizabeth's watch-dogs almost forgot the royal prisoner. She no longer seemed a pressing responsibility. James of Scotland was growing up under the guidance of his mother's bitterest enemy, the Queen of England. He was taught that Mary was a thoroughly wicked woman, and he made no effort to release her. Of course this suited Elizabeth's purpose. Mary became a legend. Young people growing up in Scotland sighed as they thought of their captive princess, and in Catholic countries she was not forgotten.

Mary had been locked up for more than eight years when one of those great waves washed over her, and she heard that Don John of Austria was coming to the rescue.

This famous Spaniard, the half-brother of the King of Spain and hero of Lepanto, planned to attack Elizabeth boldly, carry off the Queen of Scots, and (of course) marry her. It was with great confidence that Mary awaited him, for Don John was always successful. But the withering hand of fate touched him, as it seemed to touch everyone who tried to help the poor captive. Don John sickened and died in the Netherlands.

CHAPTER ELEVEN

The End

A CONQUERING ARMY, when occupying a country, always finds that one thing gets badly in the way of discipline. This is the fact that troops are human, even when they are supposed to lord it over subject peoples. In spite of the enmity that has sent their masters to war, soldiers and plain people, sooner or later, always find a way of getting on together. Today we call this friendship "fraternizing." Friendly relations between conquered people and invaders are not approved by the invaders' leaders, because they feel their men will be softened by such friendship. They fear the men will be tricked, and the enemy will rise again and throw off their yoke.

The same problem arises between prisoners and their jailers. A jailer must not be soft-hearted, if his prisoners are dangerous. At least that is what prison-keepers think. They find it very hard to strike a balance between downright cruelty and foolish softness.

Elizabeth and Cecil still worried now and then because of Mary's charming ways. They tried to find a warder for the Queen who would be strict enough to prevent her escape, yet kind and respectful enough to deal with a Queen as was proper to her rank. In Lord Shrewsbury they thought they had the ideal man. They knew he was honest and loyal to Elizabeth, and yet that he could be trusted not to insult Mary.

The Queen of Scots lived with the Shrewsburys for years, but in time the human element crept in even there and upset the balance. Mary and Lady Shrewsbury struck up a friendship at first, as they were bound to do under such intimate conditions. Then ambition began its work on Lady Shrewsbury; she tried to make plans to marry Mary or James to one of her relatives. When these plans fell through, the women quarreled.

In the meantime, it appeared that some of Mary's intrigues might be successful. The English Court suddenly took note again of their royal prisoner. Mary moved house.

It was 1585. Incredible as it must have seemed to her, Mary was forty-three. She had been a prisoner for eighteen years. Years of big and little waves had washed over her, and these, as well as the long deadly periods when nothing happened, had left their mark. After so much forced inactivity, the Queen had grown fat. She was crippled with rheumatism, in spite of the fact that Elizabeth sometimes permitted her to visit the hot baths for treatment. She spent an immense amount of time on needlework; a good many samples of her skill she sent to Elizabeth. The two Queens continued to correspond, usually in polite vein though sometimes Mary's sense of injustice boiled over and she freely expressed her indignation.

Mary's other interests (apart from intrigue)

Mary had a great fondness for her "little animals"

were her "little animals" as she called them—birds and small dogs, of which she had a great number. But still her overwhelming passion was conspiracy. It was wine to her.

Some historians blame her for this. They say she behaved very badly, and was impossible to deal with. But what else could she be expected to do? According to her mind, she was rightful Queen of England, as well as Scotland. Her destiny was to rule. She had been bred to rule; she wanted to rule: of course she bent every effort to achieve her end. Intrigue, false courtesy—it was all part of the game. Elizabeth understood this. She in her turn bent her energy to maintaining her position; her duty as she saw it was to frustrate Mary. But she understood the other Queen's mind and actions, and in reality, no matter what she said, she felt no anger at them.

What she did to Mary she did from policy, not rage.

The climax was reached this year. There was on the continent, in France and Spain, a secret society called the Catholic League. In close correspondence with it was a young Englishman named Antony Babington who had known Mary as a child when he was Lord Shrewsbury's ward. When he grew up and went to Court he met Edmund Campion, the great Catholic leader. Fired by desire to help the cause of

Catholicism, he thought at once of delivering Mary.

Sir Francis Walsingham, Elizabeth's Secretary of State, got wind of the plan, for very few of Mary's plots and intrigues escaped his vigilant eyes. He resolved to use his chances, and instead of ignoring this particular plot, which under ordinary conditions would probably have fizzled out like the others, he took a hand in it, and cunningly planted evidence. Under his indirect encouragement it grew to alarming proportions. The young men who had rallied around Antony Babington were soon plotting to commit that most treasonable of acts, the murder of Queen Elizabeth.

Carefully, Elizabeth's spies collected their evidence. Walsingham made it his business to get a copy of every missive that passed between Mary and her friends outside, including those he had himself inspired. Then he struck. In August, 1585, the youths in the conspiracy were all arrested and committed to the Tower. Under torture Babington admitted everything. He and his fellows were put to death on September 17.

Soon after that, Mary was permitted to go on one of her rare hunting parties, and while she was away Walsingham's men searched her quarters and took away her private papers. Then she, too, was placed under close arrest and sent to Fotheringay Castle, in Northamptonshire.

It was not so simple a matter to deal with the royal Mary as it had been with the young men. Even Elizabeth's ministers dared not put a queen to the torture. And at the inquiry Mary, who conducted her own defense, was a shrewd lawyer. Though she must have known the case was hopeless from the beginning, she spoke eloquently.

She admitted having corresponded with Babington. Against the testimony of the dead boys as well as of her own secretaries she could not well deny it. She admitted that she had corresponded with foreign princes. What she did not admit was that she had known of any plot against Elizabeth's life.

However, the Commission ruled unanimously that she was guilty.

It took Elizabeth more than a month to steel herself to the decision that Mary must die. However, she sent word at last to her cousin that the verdict had gone against her, and she must prepare for death. Even then Elizabeth did not sign the warrant for execution. She waited from November until February of the next year to do that.

Again, people have condemned the Queen of England for her cruelty in thus putting her cousin to long-drawn-out mental torture. But it was not cruelty that held Elizabeth back. It was the gravity of the affair. To execute a prince of the blood royal was a terrible thing. Mary's son James was to live in history as a remarkable King, for both his mother and his son, Charles I, died by execution. Even a century later, the thought of such an act horrified the world.

Besides, Elizabeth in her rare moments of simple human feeling doubtless felt sorry that she must treat Mary in such a fashion. True, they had never met face to face. True, Mary had encouraged Elizabeth's would-be murderers. But this was all in the grim game of monarchy, and the two queens had known each other, though at a distance, for a long time. They had

Elizabeth signed the warrant for Mary's death

exchanged pretty little presents and made jokes together.

So Elizabeth hemmed and hawed and left the matter out of her daily routine for months. Even at the end, she tried to get out of signing the warrant. She sent word to Mary's jailer Sir

Amyas Poulet that if he knew his duty he would in all that time have found some way "to shorten the life of the Queen." Elizabeth "taketh it most unkindly that you should cast the burden upon her, knowing as you do her indisposition to shed blood."

But Sir Amyas, too, shrank from the responsibility. Though Elizabeth had practically commanded him to do so, he would not commit murder. He replied that he was in great grief that he should have been required by his most gracious sovereign to do an act which God and the law forbade. "But God forbid that I should make so foul a shipwreck of my conscience."

The Queen of England nerved herself at last, and signed the warrant.

Even then she wouldn't face the responsibility. When everything was over, she pretended she hadn't known it was going to take place. She flew into a passion, and took it out on the nearest person, her private secretary Davison. The unfortunate man was fined and put into jail. (Sir Amyas, you see, knew what was good for him.) But later when everything had calmed down, she remitted the fine, and granted Davison a pension.

You may wonder how Mary was acting under such a tremendous strain. She behaved as we would expect: she showed magnificent courage. After the warning from Elizabeth she spent her time quietly, at her needlework or praying on her knees. With great presence of mind she made what arrangements she could, dividing her small fortune among her servants and faithful friends.

One thing she wished very much to leave clear on the record. She wanted to be sure, and she wanted the world to be sure, that she died for the Catholic faith. The Earl of Kent, who with Shrewsbury came to announce her impending death, preached at her angrily about her Church. He said she could not be allowed to live without endangering the State, the Queen of England and the Protestant religion. "Your life would be the death of our religion, your death will be its life," he said.

This made Mary happy. She felt now that she was dying for the highest cause. She was being martyred for her faith. After a long and wretched life, such a prospect filled her not with grief or fear, but only with joy.

On February 8, 1586, at eight o'clock in the morning, Mary Queen of Scots went to her death.

She dressed herself in fine clothing, with a dark red velvet petticoat under her black gown. Until the last moment before entering the execution hall, her thoughts were of her domestics, who crowded about her, weeping. Eight of her own people wished to go in with her, and when Kent and Shrewsbury tried to keep her two maids out, she promised they would not break into noisy tears. It was not the custom, the women protested, for princes to go to their deaths unattended, and they had their way.

Three hundred people were allowed in the hall to watch. In the court outside there was a great crowd; among them minstrels who played a jig, "Joan's Placket Is Torn," as the Queen walked into the hall. It was a tune usually played at the execution of witches. But this time the music was played slowly, as if it were a dirge.

Dr. Fletcher, the Dean of Peterborough, tried

With dignity Mary stood before the executioner

to preach the last words of religion to Mary and pray with her, but she refused, saying they two were not of the same faith. When in spite of this the Dean began to pray, she prayed against him, until he was silent. Then Mary prayed alone as a Catholic, using English instead of Latin, so that nobody would mistake what she was saying.

She began to take off her black outer gown, so that her neck would be bare. The executioner wanted to help her, but she waved him away with a jest, saying, "I understand this business better than you. I never had such groom of the chamber before."

She kissed her maids good-bye. She took a little gold cross off her neck and tried to give it to one of them, Jane Kennedy, but the executioner seized it, saying, "That is my right." Jane Kennedy put a gold-embroidered handkerchief over Mary's face and pinned it. Then, refusing to be bound with the cords they had ready, Mary put her head on the block, saying in Latin,

"In Thee, God, I hope. I commend myself to Thy hands."

The executioner struck, clumsily, and had to strike again. Mary was dead.

When he held up the head, the wig she had been wearing came off. Underneath, the real hair of the forty-four-year-old Queen was pure white.

During her last days Mary wrote a poem of prayer which is hauntingly lovely. People have called it strange that she should have written in such a lilting, joyful meter. But there is no doubt she was genuinely happy to die, and small wonder.

"O Domine Deus, speravi in te!
O care mi Jesu, nunc libera me!
In dura catena, in misera poena,
Languendo, gemendo, et genuflectendo,
Adoro, imploro, ut liberes me."

"Lord God, all my hopes have I rested in
Thee!
Oh Jesus, dear Jesus, at last set me free!
In captivity's chains, in misery's pains,
I languish, I anguish, and kneeling be-
fore Thee,
Adoring, implore Thee to liberate me."

CHAPTER TWELVE

Afterthought

MARY'S FORTY-FOUR YEARS were packed with sorrowful adventure. It was a tragic life, but it was more than that. While she was alive the western world, like a child growing up, took a sudden spurt forward.

Because Mary Stuart was a queen, she had to bear the brunt of these growing-pains. John Knox was her bitter enemy. Mary was a symbol of the old world where kings ruled by the superstition of divine right. Knox was the new world that thought and questioned and demanded human rights. Like many reformers he was harsh and unlovable. But he had to happen. It was bad luck for Mary that he happened to her, but change is always cruel to somebody.

Actually it was Elizabeth who killed Mary. But if we look at the whole pattern we can see that the Scottish Queen died because the day of absolute monarchs was coming to an end. Her grandson Charles I died for the same cause. Slowly, relentlessly, the mass of the people was working toward a republican form of government.

They would not have recognized the democracy they sought. But they felt the rebellious urge that was the beginning.

Mary, an absolute prince, was doomed. She died, however, upheld by the spirit of absolutism. She died proudly and confidently. We are republicans now, as we wish to be and must be, but there was beautiful courage in that death. We see the beauty and the courage, and that is why we remember Mary, Queen of Scots.

THE END

INDEX

Have you read these World Landmarks?

★

CHECK THE LIST BELOW

W-1 **The First Men in the World,** by Anne Terry White

W-2 **Alexander the Great,** by John Gunther

W-3 **The Adventures and Discoveries of Marco Polo,** by Richard J. Walsh

W-4 **Joan of Arc,** by Nancy Wilson Ross

W-5 **King Arthur and His Knights,** by Mabel L. Robinson

W-6 **Mary, Queen of Scots,** by Emily Hahn

W-7 **Napoleon and the Battle of Waterloo,** by Frances Winwar

W-8 **Royal Canadian Mounted Police,** by Richard L. Neuberger

W-9 **The Man Who Changed China,** by Pearl S. Buck

W-10 **The Battle of Britain,** by Quentin Reynolds

W-11 **The Crusades,** by Anthony West

W-12 **Genghis Khan,** by Harold Lamb

W-13 **Queen Elizabeth and the Spanish Armada,** by Frances Winwar

W-14 **Simon Bolivar,** by Arnold Whitridge

W-15 **The Slave Who Freed Haiti,** by Katharine Scherman

W-16 **The Story of Scotland Yard,** by Laurence Thompson

W-17 **The Life of Saint Patrick,** by Quentin Reynolds

W-18 **The Exploits of Xenophon,** by Geoffrey Household

W-19 **Captain Cook Explores the South Seas,** by Armstrong Sperry

W-20 **Marie Antoinette,** by Bernadine Kielty

W-21 **Shakespeare and the Globe Theatre,** by Anne Terry White

W-22 **The French Foreign Legion,** by Wyatt Blassingame

LANDMARK BOOKS

1. **The Voyages of Christopher Columbus** by Armstrong Sperry
2. **The Landing of the Pilgrims** by James Daugherty
3. **Pocahontas and Captain John Smith** by Marie Lawson
4. **Paul Revere and the Minute Men** by Dorothy Canfield Fisher
5. **Our Independence and the Constitution** by Dorothy Canfield Fisher
6. **The California Gold Rush** by May McNeer
7. **The Pony Express** by Samuel Hopkins Adams
8. **Lee and Grant at Appomattox** by MacKinlay Kantor
9. **The Building of the First Transcontinental Railroad** by Adele Nathan
10. **The Wright Brothers** by Quentin Reynolds
11. **Prehistoric America** by Anne Terry White
12. **The Vikings** by Elizabeth Janeway
13. **The Santa Fe Trail** by Samuel Hopkins Adams
14. **The Story of the U. S. Marines** by George Hunt
15. **The Lewis and Clark Expedition** by Richard L. Neuberger
16. **The Monitor and the Merrimac** by Fletcher Pratt
17. **The Explorations of Père Marquette** by Jim Kjelgaard
18. **The Panama Canal** by Robert Considine
19. **The Pirate Lafitte and the Battle of New Orleans** by Robert Tallant
20. **Custer's Last Stand** by Quentin Reynolds
21. **Daniel Boone** by John Mason Brown
22. **Clipper Ship Days** by John Jennings
23. **Gettysburg** by MacKinlay Kantor
24. **The Louisiana Purchase** by Robert Tallant
25. **Wild Bill Hickok Tames the West** by Stewart Holbrook
26. **Betsy Ross and the Flag** by Jane Mayer
27. **The Conquest of the North and South Poles** by Russell Owen
28. **Ben Franklin of Old Philadelphia** by Margaret Cousins
29. **Trappers and Traders of the Far West** by James Daugherty
30. **Mr. Bell Invents the Telephone** by Katherine Shippen
31. **The Barbary Pirates** by C. S. Forester
32. **Sam Houston, The Tallest Texan** by William Johnson
33. **The Winter at Valley Forge** by Van Wyck Mason
34. **The Erie Canal** by Samuel Hopkins Adams
35. **Thirty Seconds Over Tokyo** by Ted Lawson and Bob Considine
36. **Thomas Jefferson** by Vincent Sheean
37. **The Coming of the Mormons** by Jim Kjelgaard
38. **George Washington Carver** by Anne Terry White
39. **John Paul Jones** by Armstrong Sperry
40. **The First Overland Mail** by Robert Pinkerton
41. **Teddy Roosevelt and the Rough Riders** by Henry Castor
42. **To California by Covered Wagon** by George R. Stewart
43. **Peter Stuyvesant of Old New York** by Anna and Russel Crouse
44. **Lincoln and Douglas** by Regina Z. Kelly
45. **Robert Fulton and the Steamboat** by Ralph Nading Hill
46. **The F. B. I.** by Quentin Reynolds
47. **Dolly Madison** by Jane Mayer
48. **John James Audubon** by Margaret and John Kieran
49. **Hawaii** by Oscar Lewis
50. **War Chief of the Seminoles** by May McNeer
51. **Old Ironsides, The Fighting *Constitution*** by Harry Hansen
52. **The Mississippi Bubble** by Thomas B. Costain
53. **Kit Carson and the Wild Frontier** by Ralph Moody
54. **Robert E. Lee and the Road of Honor** by Hodding Carter
55. **Guadalcanal Diary** by Richard Tregaskis
56. **Commodore Perry and the Opening of Japan** by Ferdinand Kuhn
57. **Davy Crockett** by Stewart Holbrook
58. **Clara Barton, Founder of the American Red Cross** by Helen Dore Boylston
59. **The Story of San Francisco** by Charlotte Jackson
60. **Up the Trail from Texas** by J. Frank Dobie

WORLD
Landmark
BOOKS